PRAYING AT
EVERY TURN

Christmas
2011

To Kira + Tim

I am so thankful
that your path + my path
have come close to each
other (and for Kira + I more than
once - VTS)
as we move toward the
Center.

Love,
Hilary

Other Books by the Author

Labyrinths from the Outside In: Walking to
  Spiritual Insight — A Beginner's Guide
  (with Donna Schaper)
Complete Idiot's Guide to Sewing Illustrated
American Women Inventors
American Women Scientists
Sally Ride: Woman Astronaut
American Astronomers: Searchers and Wonderers

Books Edited by the Author

From Flicker to Flame: Women's Sermons for the
  Revised Common Lectionary, Year A, Volumes 1
  and 2
Cells: Life's Building Blocks
The Matter-Energy Cycle
Heredity: Generation to Generation
Evolving
Interdependence
Life's Diversity

PRAYING AT EVERY TURN

Meditations for Walking the Labyrinth

CAROLE ANN CAMP

A Crossroad Book
The Crossroad Publishing Company
New York

This printing: 2011

The Crossroad Publishing Company
www.CrossroadPublishing.com

The Scripture quotations contained herein are from the New Revised Standard Version Bible, copyright © 1993 by the Division of Christian Education of the National Council of the Churches of Christ in the U.S.A. Used by permission.

Printed in the United States of America

The text of this book is set in Benguiat, Triplex, and Goudy Old Style. The display faces are Worstveld Sting and Benguiat.

Cataloging-in-Publication Data is available from the Library of Congress

ISBN-10: 0-8245-2387-3
ISBN-13: 978-0-8245-2387-9

For all of my grandchildren
who are just learning how to walk
and
for all of the adults
who are just learning to walk for the first time

Contents

Week Three
WALKING THE PATH OF JESUS

Week Four
TRANSCENDENCE

"Walking" the Labyrinth

Use a pencil, pen, or your finger to follow the path of labyrinth in the above figure. Go slowly. Stay aware of your inner thoughts and feelings as you follow the path. Pause in the center, for as long as you wish, then follow the path back out. It can be helpful to read one of the meditations before or after you complete the circuits of the path.

During the Tuscany retreat, we built two labyrinths. One, on a hilltop, was created from clay roof tiles. Another, in a stone chapel, was totally ringed with glittering tea lights. But it was Gernot's teachings that led us. "Ask questions," he'd say. "Ask, what waits for me in the middle? What do I meet, deep in my soul? Do I move on? Do I follow the path? There's no right, no wrong. Just being on the way. Just keep walking. Think about what you'd like to risk in this lifetime. The path will offer everything you need. Walk, and look within."

— From the Foreword by Paula D'Arcy
to Gernot Candolini's *Labyrinths*

A SACRED WALK

You show me the path of life.
In your presence there is fullness of joy;
in your right hand are pleasures forevermore.
— Psalm 16:11

Throughout history, people have walked the ancient archetypal spirals of labyrinths as a spiritual practice. One unique aspect of the labyrinth is that one finds the center if one stays on the path. Various shaped labyrinths exist all over the world, falling into two basic general shapes popular today: the classic seven-circuit unicursal labyrinth — the most famous one found in Chartres Cathedral in France — and its earlier predecessor, the Cretan labyrinth.

Walking the path into the center of the labyrinth is a metaphor for finding one's own center or finding God. Walking out of the labyrinth is a symbol of being reborn into the world. While most people use the words "maze" and "labyrinth" interchangeably, there are many significant differences

11

between the two. Mazes are designed to confuse walkers. There are dead ends, paths that go no-where, and paths that lead in circles. The walls of the maze are often tall, thick hedges one cannot see over, which causes panic and fear. That is the whole point — to get lost and to try to figure out how to get out of the maze. In a labyrinth, there is only one path. The path leads to the center. There are no dead ends. If one stays on the path, one finds the center. One is never lost. The path into the center is also the same path back out into the world. While mazes promote fear and panic, laby-rinths provide safety and peace. The metaphor of walking a labyrinth is that if one stays on the path through all the myriad turnings, one will surely find one's center.

In the Christian tradition at some times in his-tory, the inward path represented a pilgrimage to Jerusalem. Labyrinths also represented Christ, especially those that were laid down in naves of cathedrals. Other cultures and religious traditions put their own meaning on the labyrinth. That is one of the archetypal and astonishing aspects of the labyrinth. The symbolism holds across cultures, religions, and time.

For me, the path of the labyrinth represents a spiritual journey, and the center symbolizes my center/God's center. I also believe that the path in is as important as the path out. In my experience, I always receive a gift, some insight, some feeling, some thought or idea. Sometimes the gift is a very practical solution to a problem. Other times it is more ethereal, and more difficult to put into words, but one to cherish in my heart nevertheless. Sometimes the gift is the calm that surrounds me as if I am being held in the "hollow of God's hand." Sometimes, even though I know I have been given a gift, I don't quite "get" its significance at the time — the meaning coming much later.

The purpose of this book is to help you pray the labyrinth. There are many different kinds of prayer. There are hundreds of books on or about prayer. There are prayers that many Christians know by heart like the Lord's Prayer or "Hail, Mary." There are long prayers and short prayers. There are prayers with words and there are wordless prayers. There are talking prayers and there are listening prayers. Choosing to pray is like making a commitment to focus your time and attention on growing in spirit. Walking the labyrinth is body prayer — a prayer one does with the whole body. Combining walking with some other form of prayer will deepen the peace you will experience in the center. Prayer opens up the possibility of coming face-to-face with God. When one commits oneself to the daily practice of walking prayer, one's connectedness to God grows.

Praying the labyrinth is more than just walking and praying, however. Praying the labyrinth is walking in a state of prayer. It is an attitude, not a set of words — a total surrender to God, a total relinquishment of ego. Walking in prayer is more like a state of being than an action. It doesn't matter whether you choose to say a word prayer or not. Walking prayer is the process of becoming conscious of God. It is a spiritual listening to God with your whole body.

There is no "right" way to walk in prayer, just as there is no "right" way to walk a labyrinth. It is all about finding your own path. There are no "right" words. Walking prayer is about letting go and being totally relaxed. Walking prayer is about allowing the presence of God to lead you. There is no goal. There is no expectation. There is no agenda. Just walking, allowing yourself to be led by God is enough.

As you walk the labyrinth this month, try a variety of prayer types, and find the one that works for you. Suggestions are given for each day, but they are only suggestions.

The Christian Liturgical Year

Throughout the course of human history, people have marked the changing of the seasons with celebrations and holy days. This recycling of the seasonal cycle of holy days brings meaning to daily life. For Christians, the calendar has six seasons, beginning with Advent and ending with Pentecost. Advent is a time of preparation; Christmas, Epiphany, Lent, and Easter build on the birth, life, death, and resurrection of Jesus; while the last season, Pentecost, celebrates the life of the church.

This daily meditation follows a similar pattern: the preparation, and the birth, life, death, and resurrection of Jesus. During the first week, there are meditations from the Hebrew Scriptures, or First Testament, setting the stage. During the second week, the meditations focus on birthings and re-birthings. The third week emphasizes following the path of Jesus' life. The fourth week culminates in resurrection and transformation. On some level,

it doesn't matter where you start in the book, because it is a circle, but it might be easier to start on
Day 1 of Week One. It is also not necessary to have
Day 1 be a Monday. Whatever day you begin is Day
1 of your spiritual journey.

Daily walks in the labyrinth, of course, are the
ideal. However, if you miss a day or days, don't
punish yourself. Just continue on the path.

Week One

Walking with God

Sometimes we are so busy running through our lives we forget to walk consciously through our lives. Being aware or being in a state of awareness is a curious phenomenon. The more aware one is, the more aware one becomes. One becomes more aware of miracles that happen every minute of every day. One becomes more aware of how the Holy Spirit intercedes in and intersects with our lives.

It is like tuning in a radio to find the right station to get clearer reception. The radio waves are always there, but we are unaware of them most of the time. Just because we can't hear them or see them, however, doesn't mean they are not there. As soon as we turn on the radio, as soon as we tune in for better reception, we begin to hear what was there all along.

The same is true with God. Think of God as a radio wave. It is always there. But how do we tune into God? How do we put ourselves in a more receptive state of being? How do we begin to hear God clearly and get rid of all the other static that seems to clutter our heads and hearts and souls? By choosing to practice a discipline, you have already decided to tune yourself into God.

God is always walking with us. Now it is time to walk with God — to walk with God in prayer. At some level, we can sit in a chair and still walk with God in prayer. We don't even need to walk in a labyrinth. One of my friends says, "I haven't walked an official labyrinth ever. I kind of make them up wherever I can — the backyard (sometimes while I'm cutting grass), in the woods, on the beach — and as I need them. What's the difference between 'praying' and 'just walking'? Just walking is the way I pray whether on a labyrinth or on a walk. I usually come out feeling more peaceful than when I started; it does relieve tension for me."

While for some this is true, walking a labyrinth is like fine-tuning the reception. Praying the labyrinth is making that conscious decision to say, "Yes!" to God. The metaphor of the labyrinth itself provides a new tuning. Praying while walking the labyrinth allows you to hear in ways you may never have heard before.

The Bible is a book of stories about a people walking — walking with God — walking from bondage to transcendence. In Week One, we begin our journey with seven lessons from the ancient Hebrew Scriptures.

WANDERING
IN THE WILDERNESS

Exodus 13:3, 17–18a

Moses said to the people, "Remember this day on which you came out of Egypt, out of the house of slavery, because the LORD brought you out from there by strength of hand; no leavened bread shall be eaten."

When Pharaoh let the people go, God did not lead them by way of the land of the Philistines, although that was nearer; for God thought, "If the people face war, they may change their minds and return to Egypt." So God led the people by the roundabout way of the wilderness toward the Red Sea.

The first time I walked a labyrinth I had no idea what a labyrinth was. My friend had mown one into her backyard—a yard

21

that was very large and — excuse me, Betty — very unkempt. I looked out upon the expanse of yard from the back porch and wondered how anyone could tell where the labyrinth was, let alone the path. Betty dragged me to what looked like unraked weedy grass. Even though we were in the middle of a large town, and in the middle of a fenced-in yard, I had this sinking feeling that I was about to enter a wilderness. Betty explained that all I had to do was stay on the path — the mown part between the piles of grass — and I would find the center. From my perspective, I couldn't see the design of the labyrinth or the center. At the time, I didn't know the difference between mazes and labyrinths. I thought surely I'd be lost in this maze, wandering hopelessly forever, never finding the center and never being able to get out.

MUCH OF THE EXODUS STORY is about a people wandering in the wilderness of their spiritual journey. Their story, while quite long, has a very simple outline: from bondage to wilderness to the promised land.

We are not living in 2100 B.C.E., we are not in Egypt, and none of us are slaves of the pharaoh; but we may still be in bondage. In a modern translation of this story, we may be in bondage to our work or to our relationships. We may be addicted to drugs, alcohol, money, or sex. These bondages keep us from being whole. These additions can keep us from experiencing the true peace and transcendence that God intended for us. These dead ends of the human condition keep us from finding our centers and from opening ourselves to God.

Identifying the pharaoh in our life doesn't automatically catapult us to the Promised Land, however nice that would be. We have a tendency to want to skip right from the bondage part to the Promised Land part. Why take half an hour to walk to the center of the labyrinth when one can just skip all the walking and get to the center right away?

Instead, "God led the people by the roundabout way of the wilderness." God led them by a roundabout way!

Do not be tempted to avoid the wilderness; it is a primary and very important experience. It is basic to our understanding of who we are and who our God is. It was in this wilderness experience that a very mixed-up, raggle-taggle bunch of refugees came face-to-face with God. The wilderness is not easy, but God comes through every time. God sends manna. God provides water. God promises eagles' wings.

Many biblical scholars and scientists debate endlessly about what the manna was. Quite frankly,

Who cares? What is important to remember is that the people who had taken the risk to leave their pharaohs behind, the people who were struggling in the wilderness, who were hungry, thirsty, fearful, and anxious, were fed. The people were on a spiritual journey, and they were nourished. God did not abandon them. What is important about this story is that each one of us will, in fact, get what we need for our spiritual journeys. It doesn't matter how much we complain, or how much we want to go back to the pharaoh of our addictions, or how impatient we are, God will not abandon us. All we have to do is turn away from the pharaoh and take the first step onto the path.

Once we set out on our journey, we will be nourished and nurtured along the way. The manna may not fall over us like bread from the sky; it may be as simple as seeing a white dove circling over us — the symbol of the Holy Spirit. Our thirst may be quenched by receiving a special phone call at just the right time or finding a book with a message we need to hear at that moment. Someone may send you a bouquet of iris when it's not even your birthday. The manna may float down to you on the notes of a hymn or a song on the radio, and you hear the familiar words as if for the first time, as if this music were written especially for you.

As you walk the labyrinth today, leave your metaphorical pharaoh behind and know that God will send manna from heaven to nourish you along the way.

Prayer

Holy One, give me bread for the journey, give me bread.

ON EAGLES' WINGS

Exodus 19:1–8
Isaiah 40:31

On the third new moon after the Israelites had gone out of the land of Egypt, on that very day, they came into the wilderness of Sinai.... Then Moses went up to God; the LORD called to him from the mountain, saying, "Thus you shall say to the house of Jacob, and tell the Israelites: You have seen what I did to the Egyptians, and how I bore you on eagles' wings and brought you to myself.

"Now therefore, if you obey my voice and keep by covenant, you shall be my treasured possession out of all the peoples. Indeed, the whole earth is mine, but you shall be for me a priestly kingdom and a holy nation."... So Moses came, summoned the elders of the people, and set before them all these words that the LORD had commanded him. The people all answered as one: "Everything that the LORD has spoken we will do."

But those who wait for the LORD shall renew their strength, they shall mount up with wings like eagles, they shall walk and not faint.

One Sunday I introduced a period of silence into the worship service. I thought being silent for five minutes would be a good start. At about two minutes, I could hear the rustling of papers and the clearing of throats. I ended the silence in less than three minutes. I was bemused by the fact that in the meditation group I led, people often complained that thirty minutes was too short. How can it be that three minutes is too long and thirty minutes is too short? Being on a spiritual journey is a long, slow process. Walking a labyrinth is a long, slow process. Sometimes the journey seems too long, and sometimes it seems too short.

YESTERDAY, WE LEFT the Israelites wandering in the wilderness, having just left slavery and seeking the Promised Land. They are in the desert — hot, discouraged — and they are walking. Walking toward a promised land none of them have ever seen. They want to go back — to give up. There are days when they wonder where they will get enough strength to go on. Every ounce of their energy has been used up. It doesn't seem possible that they will be able to take another step.

Yesterday you left your own pharaoh behind. You took the risk and stepped out into the wilderness. The journey may have seemed too long, the path too convoluted. You may have wondered whatever happened to the geometry axiom that states that the shortest distance between two points is a straight line. You may have even given up and not continued on to find the center.

As the Israelites struggle to walk their path, they hear God somewhere on the edge of their consciousness: You have seen what I have done, and how I bore you on eagles' wings and brought you to myself.

Oh!, the longing, the incredible yearning to be brought to God's self!

There really are no words to describe the ecstasy — the intense feelings of joy — that happens when we know that God is holding us as if in the palm of a hand, knowing that we are being carried as if on eagles' wings into the heart of God.

For our friends in the desert, forty years of putting one foot in front of the other seems like a long time.

Walking, walking, walking toward the promise. God gives them manna and water along the way — reassurance that God is still with them, guiding them on.

Every day we keep putting one foot in front of the other. Walking, walking, walking toward the promise. We catch glimpses, moments when we experience God's presence. But regardless of how fleeting these manna moments are, they are enough to give us the hope and the strength we need to take that next step. They are enough to renew our spiritual resources when we run dry. Those who hope in the Lord will renew their strength. They will soar on wings like eagles; they will run and not grow weary, they will walk and not be faint.

In the Exodus experience, a truly amazing event occurs. God says that if the people obey God's voice and keep the covenant, they shall be a holy people. Holiness is not a privileged status or position. Holiness is a state of being, a way one is in the world, a way one acts in the world. The actions of the people of God are different from those of the people around them. God's people are expected to act from a position of kindness, generosity of spirit, abundance, joy, and justice.

The people say that big "Yes" to God because they remember what it felt like when God bore them forth on eagles' wings, from slavery to freedom, from being nobody to being somebody, from being no people to being a holy people.

As you walk the labyrinth today, toward the center, toward your center, toward your promise, reflect on how God is bearing you on eagles' wings into wholeness and holiness.

Prayer

Holy One, thank you for bearing me up on eagles' wings.

COMPANIONS
ALONG THE WAY

Ruth 1:16–18

But Ruth said, "Do not press me to leave you or to turn back from following you! Where you lodge, I will lodge; your people shall be my people, and your God my God. Where you die, I will die — there will I be buried. May the LORD do thus and so to me, and more as well, if even death parts me from you!" When Naomi saw that she was determined to go with her, she said no more to her.

I have walked a labyrinth in Florida with my mother, one in Chicago with my sister, and one in California with my daughter. I caught glimpses, fleeting moments of specialness with each of them. We slowly walked, sometimes coming toward

each other, sometimes going away from each other, and sometimes walking parallel to each other, but on different parts of
the path, each of us on our own journey, yet linked by some
invisible cord, journeying toward God. No words were spoken,
just the ongoing meetings and partings to be together in God.
Because of the design of the labyrinth, it is possible to be walking shoulder to shoulder with someone, yet on different parts
of the labyrinth. I remember as my sister and I walked along
touching shoulders, she on her path, I on mine, the pain of sep-
aration as my path turned away from hers. I wanted to go with
her. I wanted her to come with me. We stayed on our own paths,
passed by each other, walked close to each other many more
times. Eventually, we met again, this time in the center, no bar-
riers between us, just a peace and tranquility that can only be
described as home with God.

THERE ARE AT LEAST three different ways to walk
in a labyrinth. While uniquely different, each experience provides its own gift of insight. The first way
is to walk totally alone. The second way is to walk
while many other strangers are walking. The third
way is to walk with a friend or loved one.

In earlier chapters of this story of Ruth and
Naomi, Naomi said: Go back to your mother's
house! Ruth was of a different culture and religion.
The journey back to Naomi's home was long and

arduous and may even have been dangerous for Ruth. At the beginning of every person's spiritual journey, the decision to leave our "mother's house" is the first step.

There is an interesting conundrum here because the first step to truly coming home is to leave home. Ruth and Naomi are choosing to journey together for a while, even though each one is on a different phase of her own personal story.

Ruth is going to Bethlehem for the first time, while Naomi is returning home after a long sojourn in a foreign land. Ruth turns toward Bethlehem and leaves everything behind. We don't have to leave everything behind or even forget everything. But for this walking, as we journey toward our spiritual home, symbolized by the labyrinth, we can safely place our worries, fears, and challenges by the side of the labyrinth and walk unburdened toward our center.

Naomi chooses to begin a new phase in her spiritual journey by returning home. Naomi knows where home was. She also knew some of the dangers, toils, and snares that lay before her. In the Exodus story, thousands of people set off together. In this story, however, the two women only had each other.

Sometimes along the way we meet someone who asks to travel with us for a while. In this case, Ruth chooses to accompany Naomi on the journey. Traveling companions for our spiritual journeys are very important and very special. Often we have many different traveling companions, some that last a lifetime, and some that come into our lives for only a short time, for a specific purpose, and then continue on their own journey.

Ruth chose a companion for part of her journey. She also chose to experience a different view of God. Naomi's God had a different name than Ruth's God. Ruth was choosing to look at God from a different perspective, with different eyes. She was willing to submerge herself in a different culture with different norms and different rituals in order to come to a more complete understanding of God and God's relationship with her.

Ruth and Naomi were ready to walk in faith. Ruth chose to love Naomi and walk with her toward an unknown future, a future filled with infinite possibilities. When she committed herself to Naomi, she was choosing to have Naomi as her traveling companion for this part of her journey.

The friendship of Ruth and Naomi began in silence as they turned and walked out into the desert.

As companions of the way, they walked and walked and walked. They were linked together by some ultimate mystery of love. Traveling companions offer each other many different gifts along the way.

For your walk today, find a traveling companion, someone who will be able to walk with you and share experiences of God with you and with whom you can share yours. Find someone who is willing to go out into the desert with you, someone who is willing to be part of your spiritual journey. As you walk, be ready to catch glimpses of God through the gifts given to you by your traveling companion.

Symbolically, leave your "mother's home," continue your journey to your new home, and "come home."

Prayer

Thank you for the gift of [companion's name] in my life.

BESIDE STILL WATERS

Psalm 23

The LORD is my shepherd, I shall not want. He makes me lie down in green pastures; he leads me beside still waters; he restores my soul. He leads me in right paths for his name's sake. Even though I walk through the darkest valley, I fear no evil; for you are with me; your rod and your staff — they comfort me. You prepare a table before me in the presence of my enemies; you anoint my head with oil; my cup overflows. Surely goodness and mercy shall follow me all the days of my life, and I shall dwell in the house of the LORD my whole life long.

One day at sunset on a beach on Cape Cod in Massachusetts, several of us had drawn a labyrinth in the sand. Even in its temporariness, the labyrinth beckoned. As I walked, the sun created the most spectacular display as it set over Nantucket Sound. The wind had died down to a whisper. Tiny waves, barely perceptible, kissed the shore. With each step I took, I could feel the stresses and strains of my life slip away into the sand beneath my feet. The gentlest feather of a breeze, the breath of God, brushed my cheek. God was by my side. No doubts! God was with me on my journey. When I reached the center of the labyrinth, I sat for a while beside the still waters as my soul was restored. God is my guide on my path—the path of my life.

ONE OF THE REASONS that Psalm 23 is so popular is that the psalmist has absolute trust in God. There are no maybes here. There are no what-ifs. There is no question about the existence of God. The Lord is my shepherd. God is my shepherd. The psalmist doesn't say, "The Lord was my shepherd," or "Some day the Lord might be my shepherd." The psalmist says, "Now, right now, the Lord is my shepherd." And that "now" extends into time in all directions. No doubt, no questions, absolute and total trust. God is my shepherd.

A modern interpretation of the word "shepherd" is "a companion along the way." No matter where life's journey takes us, even if we wander into the darkest valleys, God is our companion along the way. Because God is our traveling companion, we lack nothing. God breathed into us at the beginning of our life, and the breath of God is what sustains us through our lives. The breath of God comes from eternity, flows into us for a small amount of earth time, and continues to flow on into eternity. Our bodies house the breath of God for some undetermined amount of time. We are part of the breath of God, and the breath of God is a part of each of us. When we die, the breath of God that was part of us continues. Whether we live or whether we die, we are never separated from the breath of God.

Sheep occasionally get themselves into perilous situations, like when they roll over into a hole and cannot get back on their feet by themselves. The more they struggle, the worse they make their situation. They run the risk of dying if they continue to struggle. One of the tasks of a good shepherd is to pick up the sheep and put it back down on its feet on its path. God restores our soul in the same way. When we have gotten ourselves into a place where we are stuck and cannot stand up any longer, and when the more we struggle, the worse it gets, God brings us back to life. God sets us upright on the path again. Then God leads us beside the still waters — a place of absolute calm and peace.

This time alone with God is a time to sit still, to experience the surrounding love of God. Just to be.

When one walks in prayer, one is connected to God at an incredibly deep level. If we don't stay connected to God, how are we going to get through the busyness of our lives? Gasoline doesn't get into our automobiles by magic. We have to go to the gas station and put in the gas. We are like our cars, except our life-giving energy comes from God. If we don't take the time to let God nourish us, we run the risk of running out of gas in a most inconvenient place.

To add depth to your understanding of the psalms, try different translations of the same psalm on consecutive labyrinth walks.

> The Lord is my shepherd, I have everything I
> need
> He lets me rest in fields of green grass
> And leads me to quiet pools of green water.
> He gives me new strength.
> He guides me in the right paths, as he has
> promised.
> Even if I go through the deepest darkness,
> I will not be afraid, Lord, for you are with me.
> Your shepherd's rod and staff protect me.
> You prepare a banquet for me,

Where all my enemies can see me;
You welcome me as an honored guest
And fill my cup to the brim.
I know that your goodness and love will be
     with me all my life;
And your house will be my home as long as
     I live.   — Psalm 23, GNB

Today as you walk the labyrinth, know that God is your traveling companion. If you stumble and fall, God will pick you up. If you stray off the path, God will gently put you back on the path. Allow God to lead you lovingly and gently to the quiet waters. Close your eyes and allow one of the lines of the psalm to come into your mind. Use that phrase as your mantra for the inward journey.

Prayer

Lead me beside the still waters.

WALKING IN GOD'S WAY

1 Kings 2:1–4

When David's time to die drew near, he charged his son Solomon, saying: "I am about to go the way of all the earth. Be strong, be courageous, and keep the charge of the LORD your God, walking in his ways and keeping his statutes, his commandments, his ordinances, and his testimonies, as it is written in the law of Moses, so that you may prosper in all that you do and wherever you turn. Then the LORD will establish his word that he spoke concerning me: 'If your heirs take heed to their way, to walk before me in faithfulness with all their heart and with all their soul....'"

"Don't wander too far off! We'll meet you here at noon." These were parting words as my friends the Clarks drove off to check out Santa Fe's flea market. I'd opted instead for some intown gallery time. However, standing there in the cool shadow of St. Francis Cathedral, I questioned my choice. Already tourist traffic swarmed along the streets and sidewalks. On that fast-warming July day, those galleries were sure to be packed.

No matter. Forget the galleries. One way not to wander off was to stay put, I thought, turning away from downtown and taking the steps to the St. Francis courtyard. Off to my left an unusual sculpture immediately caught my eye. A dancing monk, an angel version of St. Francis himself perhaps? With outstretched wings for arms and closed eyes, he seemed poised there, mid-step, barefoot and on tiptoe above a pool of fountain water. Smiling at his clearly blissful posture, I walked around him. It was then that I noticed the labyrinth.

How had I missed it? Right there between the formal cathedral steps and the monk's joyful presence lay lovely concentric circles of stone, artfully set level with the pavement. For a moment I hesitated. Did I really want to spend my time in Santa Fe walking in circles? Actually, yes. With that saintly sprite as my visual partner, I not only walked the walk, but I did so with a spring in my step and, frankly, with a song in my heart. It didn't seem foolish at all. In fact, I felt almost swept away, gradually transported above the maddening crowd not a hundred yards away.

By the time my "dance" with St. Francis was over, the labyrinth was bathed in midday sunlight, I felt warmed through, and my ride arrived. "Well, you didn't wander far," the Clarks claimed, as I climbed into their air-conditioned car. "You'd be surprised," I said.

DAVID IS LYING on his deathbed talking to his son, Solomon. David tells Solomon to be strong and courageous and to walk in the ways of God. What does it mean to walk in ways of God? There are many answers to this question, along with many ambiguities. God calls us to walk on the path God intended for us to walk on.

One possibility is to hold up your personal struggle in the mirror. Allow the different aspects of the struggle to be reflected against those qualities that we have been told in various other stories in the Bible are pleasing to God, such as deep truth, justice, and love. In order to walk in God's way, we are to equip ourselves with courage, courage not as a warrior going to battle, but courage to seek deeper truth, courage to stand for justice, and courage to live a life of unconditional love. Walking in God's way is not going out for a gentle stroll, but rather a journey of wrestling with important issues.

Seeking the will of God is sometimes frustrating and sometimes even difficult. Very few of us get burning bushes or neon signs blinking on and off, "This is the will of God. This is the will of God."

Seeking the will of God is a constant and conscious task. The Good News is that we are not left on our own to discover the will of God. Many have gone before us. Stories, both ancient and modern, abound about others who have walked in ways of God. We must also remember that there are no shortcuts. Like the labyrinth, the path is long and there are no shortcuts.

We are to be constant in prayer, alert and willing to persevere. As we grasp spiritual truths and seek to apply these truths to our lives on a regular basis, we will discover more of the divine intent. We will soon come to realize that the will of God has more to do with who a person is and is becoming than where the person was and what the person was doing.

God calls us to walk on the path God intended for us to walk on, and God is walking the walk with us.

Take one of your life's struggles with you as you walk the labyrinth today. Metaphorically, hold it in God's mirror. Allow the light of God to reflect deep truth, justice, and love back to you. Walk in the ways of God.

Prayer

Let me walk in the ways of truth, justice, and love.

HERE IS THE ROAD — FOLLOW IT!

Isaiah 30:19–21

Truly, O people in Zion, inhabitants of Jerusalem, you shall weep no more. He will surely be gracious to you at the sound of your cry; when he hears it, he will answer you. . . . Your Teacher will not hide himself any more, but your eyes shall see your Teacher. And when you turn to the right or when you turn to the left, your ears shall hear a word behind you, saying, "This is the way; walk in it."

The labyrinth requires many, many turns. These are not tentative, not gradual, but "about-faces," significant changes of direction. Not just the eyes, but the whole body has to cooperate and get the turn made. The turns require a little

45

bit of discomfort and refinding of balance...and the path goes on.

CONVERSION MEANS: to turn around; to turn 180 degrees; to do an about-face. Conversion is a turning to face God. Even if you have truly believed in God your whole life, even if you have never doubted the existence of God in your life, today is an opportunity to turn and face God, not just once but many times. This is the day to tune in to God and listen. Whether you turn to the right or to the left, your ears will hear a voice behind you, saying, "This is the way; walk in it."

Today with each turning of the labyrinth, imagine yourself turning back to face God, to see God's face.

Prayer

Here, oh my God, I see thee face-to-face.

WALKING HUMBLY WITH GOD

Micah 6:1–6

"With what shall I come before the LORD, and bow myself before God on high? Shall I come before him with burnt offerings, with calves a year old? Will the LORD be pleased with thousands of rams, with ten thousands of rivers of oil? Shall I give my firstborn for my transgression, the fruit of my body for the sin of my soul?" He has told you, O mortal, what is good; and what does the LORD require of you but to do justice, and to love kindness, and to walk humbly with your God?

One day I got new glasses. I put them on and I was astounded. I hadn't realized until I put the new glasses on how much I

couldn't see without them. I hadn't realized what I was missing. Before I put on the glasses, I thought that I was seeing just
fine. But when I put my new glasses on, I realized that my vision
had really been blurred.

JOSEPH CAMPBELL, author of *The Power of Myth*,
says that the purpose of life is to follow your bliss.
As humans, we tend to look for our bliss in all the
wrong places. We look to power, prestige, money,
material possessions, and even to relationships.
Some people try to find bliss in alcohol or drugs
and even in work or physical fitness.

But bliss doesn't come from outside to the inside.
Bliss is already within each of us. All we have to do is
to learn how to access it. Again, it is like tuning in a
radio to get a clearer sound. One way to experience
true bliss is to walk humbly with God.

The first step is to realize that the only thing that
really matters is the power that comes to us from
God. The Christian conundrum is that the way to
independence lies through dependence, and the
way to freedom lies through surrender. But the dependence is on God, and the surrender is to God.
There is a very fine line and an enormous difference
between giving up and giving up to God; between

being dependent and being dependent on God; between surrendering and surrendering to God.

First, there is the aspect of bliss that comes when we recognize our deepest need and discover that God fulfills that deepest need. Second, there is the aspect of bliss that comes from living a life in mercy, in purity of heart, in making peace and doing justice. The third aspect of bliss happens when we freely choose to stand with God, no matter what. "No matter what" may mean risking one's job, risking one's security of family and relationships, and possibly even risking one's life. When we follow in God's footsteps we will know the joy of bliss.

When we walk humbly with God, our attitudes change, our lives change, and we see with different eyes — like having a new pair of glasses. That's how it is with God and with us. We go through our lives thinking we see just fine, but we don't until we choose to walk with God.

God's mercy is endless, and every day we are given a chance to turn away from the ways of death to the ways of life, from the ways of despair to the ways of hope and joy. Every day we have a chance to say "Yes!" to God. Today is always the first day of the rest of our lives. Today we can choose to make Micah's requirements our requirements. Today we can choose again to do justice, love mercy, and to walk in total obedience to our God.

Prayer

Lead me, Lord, lead me in thy righteousness. Make thy ways plain before my face. For it is Thou, Lord, that makes me dwell in safety.

Week Two

Beginnings and Endings

Beginnings and endings happen every day and every minute of every day. Our lives are a constant cycle of endings and beginnings. In countries and cultures that use the Julian calendar, new beginnings start on January 1 with New Year's resolutions. In some ancient calendars, new beginnings start at the end of October with the celebration of the end of the harvest season, while others start on the first day of spring with the vernal equinox and the planting season.

In the Christian calendar, at least liturgically, new beginnings start on the first day of Advent. It is sad that in some Christian traditions, one hears only the lessons from the first chapters of Matthew and Luke in the Advent-Christmas season. In December, when many are so busy, there is no time to listen! Jesus' birthing day stories are also so familiar and so enmeshed in childhood memories of Christmases past that we don't hear the message that is there for us today. The stories are so familiar, they have become static, like the carved nativity figures that we take out once a year and put on our mantels or windowsills, only to be wrapped up and put away with all the other Christmas decorations.

Our relationship with God is not static — secure and forever, Yes! — but not static. Our relationship with God is always changing, growing, evolving. The beginning of the Christian year is a time of darkness, a time of gestation, and a time of new beginnings. Now is the time to prepare for the miracle of new birth that is going to come to you again.

Even if you are starting your labyrinth walks of Week Two in the middle of August, it doesn't matter. This week is a week of letting go of the old, of going into the darkness, of new beginnings. It is okay to sing "Joy to the World" in May. It is okay to seek the Light from the guiding star in July or October.

As you walk the labyrinth this week, walk as if you have never been here before. Treat each walk as the first step of your spiritual journey. Prepare yourself to begin again.

Many of the lessons this week are the stories we hear at the Christmas pageant or at the midnight Christmas Eve service or Mass. As you walk and listen and pray this week, allow these almost too familiar stories to give you new gifts of enlightenment.

WALKING
IN DARKNESS

Isaiah 9:2–3a

The people who walked in darkness have seen a great light; those who lived in a land of deep darkness — on them light has shined. You have multiplied the nation, you have increased its joy; they rejoice before you as with joy at the harvest.

It was dark. At least a hundred people flowed out of the church service commemorating the first anniversary of the 9/11 attacks. Across the street, a labyrinth, whose path was marked by tiny candles, invited us to walk the walk. I wondered how we were all going to fit. The first to arrive at the labyrinth stepped onto the path to the beat of Native American drummers. More and more people followed. By the time I started my labyrinth journey, others were already returning, forming a circle around the edge of the labyrinth, the light from the labyrinth candles reflecting on their faces. As I walked, hope of peace grew in me as more and more people reflected that labyrinth light, that hope for peace in the world.

DARK AND LIGHT have a symbiotic relationship. You can't have one without the other. In spite of what we have been taught, dark is not bad and only light is good. There is no value judgment. Spiritual gifts come from both the times of light and the times of dark.

If you are standing in the noonday sun, you would barely notice a tiny candle flame. However, if you are standing in the dark of night, that same tiny candle will light your way. We sometimes think that the dark is negative, while the light is positive. It is true that the light is good and positive; it is equally true that the dark is good and positive, but in a different way.

The daily cycle of night-dark and day-light; or the monthly moon cycle of dark new moon and bright full moon; or the seasonal cycle of long nights of winter darkness and long days of summer light — all constantly remind us of the relationship between dark and light. The cycle goes on and on:

out of the darkness comes light; following the light comes dark.

Many mystics talk about the dark night of the soul — the time of total nakedness before God, the time of struggling with one's unique demons. Most of us don't look forward to this nightmare time, yet it is this same darkness that shines light on our path.

It is easier to find metaphors for the beginnings of things — with seeds and daffodils, the butterflies of spring, and warm summer breezes. So why did the church liturgists pick the end of November, the grayest month in the Northern Hemisphere, to start the Christian year? Perhaps they believed that it is necessary to go into the darkness first. How else can one see the small flicker of hope shining on some distant horizon far away on the very edge of our vision?

Walking in darkness is about walking in hope. It is difficult to walk in hope in the hard times, in the dark times of our lives. Yet it is in these very times that the light of our hope makes the most differ-ence. It is our work to remind the world that we can have peace in our time and that lions and lambs will eat together. It is by our steadfastness to the vision of shalom that the world may have that tiny flicker of hope.

The Christmas stories take place in the dark of the night — better for the shepherds to see the light of the angels, better for the wise ones to follow their star. It is no accident that the ones who decided where Christmas should be placed in the calendar chose the darkest time of the year where they lived in the Northern Hemisphere. In the silent holy night, on the clearest of midnights, the greatest of lights dawned on humanity. It is true: when people walk in darkness, they will see a great light.

Every spiritual journey is a journey to Easter — walking the story of our salvation from conception to the transcendence of the resurrection. Walking through the advent of our lives gives us time to reflect on how we are living God's gift of life to us. It is a time to reflect about how we are in relationship to God and all of God's creation. This is a time when we open ourselves once more to the hope of God's coming again into our midst.

In that darkness, listen. Listening to the dark does not mean you will actually hear a voice talking to you, although some people do hear a still small voice in their minds. Some people see images in their mind's eye. Some just have a feeling. The five senses with which you come to understand and know the outer world are mirrored in your inner world. We are familiar with terms like "inner sight" or "insight." The inner world is not limited to only one sense, inner sight. All five senses are mirrored inwardly. In addition to inner sight, we are blessed with inner hearing, inner touch, inner smell, and even inner taste. When you go into your inner world or your center, allow yourself to experience all of your inner senses. The more you practice listening with all of your inner senses in the darkness of your center, the deeper you will go into your center of being.

Getting ready is as important as that which we are getting ready for. Today we are preparing for God's promise to be fulfilled. We are making a place/space for God in our lives. Remember life is a journey, not a destination. How we do our getting ready is incredibly important.

If it is possible to walk your labyrinth in the dark or semi-dark, walk in the dark tonight. Before you begin your walk, place lighted candles on the lines of your labyrinth path. You may also want to place candles in the center of the labyrinth, so that you are constantly walking toward the light.

Prayer

Holy One, be the light for my path this day [night].

PREGNANT WITH POSSIBILITY

Luke 1:39–45

In those days Mary set out and went with haste to a Judean town in the hill country, where she entered the house of Zechariah and greeted Elizabeth. When Elizabeth heard Mary's greeting, the child leaped in her womb. And Elizabeth was filled with the Holy Spirit and exclaimed with a loud cry, "Blessed are you among women, and blessed is the fruit of your womb. And why has this happened to me, that the mother of my Lord comes to me? For as soon as I heard the sound of your greeting, the child in my womb leaped for joy. And blessed is she who believed that there would be a fulfillment of what was spoken to her by the Lord."

Having heard about the opportunity to walk a labyrinth for the first time, I looked forward to the experience without any preconceptions about how it would feel. The floor of the familiar room, with all its furniture back against the wall, was fully covered with a canvas labyrinth. The leader invited us to walk at our own pace. I had known most of the other walkers for years and years. As we walked alone, but also together — some beside, some ahead, some in the opposite direction — I was astonished by the intensity of the feelings of community I felt with them. My labyrinth walk that day, while less inwardly focused than it is today, was one of the beginning steps on my spiritual journey.

ANYONE WHO HAS GIVEN BIRTH knows and can witness to the fact that giving birth is a great joy, but it is not without pain or struggle and a great deal of mess. Babies don't just slide neatly out of women smelling of Johnson's baby powder, snuggly clothed in a new snow-white layette. Likewise, giving birth to the Holy Child within us is a great joy, but it is not without pain and struggle and even some messiness.

This is a time of preparing, preparing for the birth of our Holy Child, preparing for the miracles that God has for each of us. This is a time of waiting, waiting, to receive the Spirit. Whether you have ever been pregnant or not, try to imagine that you are pregnant now. It doesn't matter if you are a male or a female, gay or straight, single or partnered, young or old. It doesn't matter whether you have a womb or not. Imagine planting a seed of joy in your heart. Feel the tiniest little giggle deep, deep inside of you. Put your hands on your heart and feel the movement jumping about within you. Feel the joy growing inside of you.

Many pregnant women experience morning sickness or afternoon sickness, some even all-day sickness. For many this is the down side of pregnancy. Morning sickness is not a pleasurable part of being pregnant, but we can use it as a metaphor for cleansing our bodies in preparation for the birthing we are about to experience. Whatever it is that is causing your morning sickness, your stress, your headache, neckache, or backache, throw it up. Throw it up to God.

Let go of the blind parts of yourself, the parts that you don't want to see. Open your eyes to the Christ in each person you meet. Let go of the deaf parts of yourself, the part of you that really would rather not hear what is going on. Begin to hear the music of the angels floating throughout the universe. Let the music surge through your body; allow your feet to tapdance a little to the sounds of being alive.

Have you ever noticed how pregnant women walk, sort of tilted back, stomach pointing to the sky? As you walk today, walk with your heart pointing to the sky. Remember the seed you are carrying is growing in your heart. Think about being pregnant and walking tilted back so your heart is what goes forth first. Your heart is what greets the sky and greets the world. Be pregnant with joy. Let this joy grow and grow and grow within you.

Life is a series of hopes and waiting. We continue to wait for God's promise to be fulfilled. As in pregnancy, nothing of value comes into being without a period of quiet incubation: not a healthy baby, a loving relationship, a reconciliation, a new understanding, or a work of art. Brewing, baking, simmering, fermenting, ripening, germinating, gestating are the processes of becoming, and they are symbolic of that which is necessary for transformation.

Prepare room, prepare for the event that will change your life forever. With each turning of the labyrinth, turn towards God. When we allow the

Spirit of God to dwell within us and to grow within us, our lives change. When we give birth to the Holy Spirit that is within us, our lives change. When we say "Yes" to being co-creators with God, our lives change. There is no getting around it. When Jesus was born, the whole world changed. When the spirit within us is born, our whole world changes. One of the things we have to be prepared for, once we become pregnant with joy, is that nothing will be the same again.

Through the work of God in our hearts, we are transformed to live in a different way. Through this power, we are united and sent forth to bear witness to the Light in the world. When we live and share our faith, we are freed from greed and hatred that rules the world around us. We become servants of the living God. That's what the living God means: God's love being enacted in the lives of real people.

All of us, male or female, can be a womb. Within this womb, at any moment, the Holy Spirit can unite with us as individuals to bring something new to birth in us. Just as Elizabeth gave birth to John, which means graciousness, and Mary gave birth to Jesus, which means God within, we also can give birth to graciousness and the Spirit within us.

Prayer

Holy Spirit, send your angel to fertilize the seed of new life and joy within me.

MARY AND HER GOD

Luke 1:46—57

And Mary said, "My soul magnifies the Lord, and my spirit rejoices in God my Savior, for he has looked with favor on the lowliness of his servant. Surely, from now on all generations will call me blessed; for the Mighty One has done great things for me, and holy is his name. His mercy is for those who fear him from generation to generation. He has shown strength with his arm; he has scattered the proud in the thoughts of their hearts. He has brought down the powerful from their thrones, and lifted up the lowly; he has filled the hungry with good things, and sent the rich away empty. He has helped his servant Israel, in remembrance of his mercy, according to the promise he made to our ancestors, to Abraham and to his descendants forever." And Mary remained with her about three months and then returned to her home.

I don't know why I did it, but I searched for the Rosary beads that a friend gave me long ago. I hadn't prayed the Rosary for years. I found them deep in the back of my bureau drawer. I decided to "Do the Rosary" as I walked the labyrinth that day. As I walked and prayed and prayed and walked, I was carried into that time long, long ago, when two cousins met, each pregnant. I could hear Elizabeth saying to Mary, "Hail Mary, full of grace." As I walked and prayed, prayed and walked, the grace of God began to fill me and surround me, even me. I was transformed.

I HAPPEN TO BELIEVE that Luke gave Mary some of the most radical words in the Bible to say:

- God has scattered the proud.
- God has put down the mighty from their thrones.
- God has exalted those of low degree.
- God has filled the hungry with good things.
- God has sent the rich away empty.

That is an incredibly radical view of God. What Mary is saying is that God is on the side of the poor. God is with the marginalized. God is with the people who the rest of society scorns, and God is with those who suffer oppression because of unjust laws. In our culture and in our time in history those people are battered women, children suffering from sexual and physical abuse, widows and orphans, peoples of color, gays and lesbians, the poor, victims of war, and people suffering from AIDS.

Why do you suppose Mary's God had her wandering about in the desert on a donkey, when she was nine months pregnant? Why do you suppose Mary's God had her give birth to her baby in a manger in a stable with animals?

Let's face it. That was a very weird thing for Mary's God to do. And Mary's God says some pretty weird things too. Mary's God is the same God who through the prophets says that the poor will receive good tidings; people who are captive will be set free and the rich have to stop plundering the helpless. This God also says through Micah, "They shall beat their swords into plowshares, and their spears into pruning hooks; nation shall not lift up sword against nation, neither shall they learn war any more" (4:3).

I think Mary's God is radical. The word "radical" sounds like one of those quasi-dirty words, so I looked the word up in the dictionary, and it

says, "Reaching to the center or ultimate source."
Think about that. A radical person could be someone who is reaching to the center or searching for
the ultimate source.

So how can we all be radical? How can we go to
the center, our centers, in this time of violence and
war? Where do we search for the ultimate source?

Part of the answer, at least, is here in this story. All
those who choose to be radical will have to search
for their own ultimate source. I think I'm going
with Mary's God. I would rather work for peace
through love than work for war through killing. I
would rather find my security in a stable with the
animals than with a nuclear warhead. I would rather
find an automobile that gets more miles to the gal-
lon than have anyone killed for an oil field. I would
rather try to live in hope than live in fear. I would
rather risk serving a meal to one or two people who
might not really need it than to risk not serving a
meal to one family who is hungry. I would like to
be able to stand against violence, war, and hatred.
I would like to be able to stand for love, forgiveness,
joy, singing, and dancing.

Each of us is on our own spiritual journey. Each
of us has to choose our God. Each of us has to
find our own center and our own ultimate source

of being. Our choices will be different, and our individual choices might even change over time. I am choosing to walk with Mary and Mary's God. Choose to have Mary's words be your words. Say to yourself: My soul magnifies the Lord, and my spirit rejoices in God, for God has regarded the low estate of this servant, and God who is mighty has done great things for me, and holy is God's name.

For today's walk, use the phrase "My soul glorifies the Lord and my spirit rejoices in God" as a mantra. Repeat the phrase over and over as you walk.

Prayer

Holy Spirit, guide my feet as I walk and my heart as I pray.

GOING HOME

Luke 2:1–7

In those days a decree went out from Emperor Augustus that all the world should be registered. This was the first registration and was taken while Quirinius was governor of Syria. All went to their own towns to be registered. Joseph also went from the town of Nazareth in Galilee to Judea, to the city of David called Bethlehem, because he was descended from the house and family of David. He went to be registered with Mary, to whom he was engaged and who was expecting a child. While they were there, the time came for her to deliver her child. And she gave birth to her firstborn son. . . .

I spent the weekend at an unstructured retreat. On my fourth and final walk of the labyrinth, I discovered that it had given structure to my retreat. In my journal I wrote: It's now raining, a cold drizzle, rapidly becoming a steady rain, but I'm walking anyway. It's like coming home. The labyrinth has become the anchor of my retreat. I rediscover and accept that I came with all I need and I return with all I need. I am on the right path. At an intensely profound level I know what the psalmist meant, "The Presence is my Shepherd, I lack nothing that I want."

GOING HOME is one of the major themes in sacred writings, especially in the stories of the Hebrew and Christian scriptures: Naomi and Ruth, Moses, Joseph and his brothers, the "prodigal" son, the three Magi, and Mary and Joseph. Many stories about people walking home! Mary and Joseph go home in two directions though — first to Bethlehem and then back to Nazareth.

When they go home to Bethlehem, Mary and Joseph experience a great cosmic event. They give birth to the God-within-themselves and are reborn. Angels sing so loudly that mere mortals hear them. Three magicians and their retinue visit them. The magi shower them with valuable gifts, and they, the magi, come face-to-face with God. Everyone, from shepherds living in poverty to the richest in the land, share a transcendent moment. Even the animals share in the experience. Stars shine brighter than they have ever shone before. Everyone goes home transformed. No one will ever be the same again.

After this momentous and history-altering birthing, Mary and Joseph go on another journey: they walk the long way home to Nazareth.

Their journeys are symbolized in the labyrinth path. The first half of the labyrinth journey is to walk to the center, as if going home to Bethlehem. Going home, home to the center, one's center, God's center! Home, where one was born and can be reborn again. Home, where cosmic events happen. Home, where one can give birth to the God-within. Home, where angel voices can be heard above the traffic noises, the city sounds, the roar of airplanes. Home, where God's gifts are waiting. Home, where in the midst of the chaos of life and living, one can come face-to-face with God, and it will be okay. Home, where it doesn't matter whether one is rich or poor, gay or straight, male or female, where it doesn't matter what political party one belongs to. Home, the center, one's center, God's center. Home, where one will never be the same again.

Of course, one can't stay washed in this starlight forever. One has to walk out of the labyrinth, taking the long way home to Nazareth, where babies die

from malnutrition; women are beaten by their part-
ners; the human family is divided and set against
itself in a myriad of ways, and instead of elephants
and donkeys sitting down together, brother takes
up arms against brother.

Both homes are real. What is also real is the
journey — the taking of one step at a time. The
experience of home in the center of the labyrinth
enables and gives us the strength and peace we
need to live at our other home in the world. It is no
accident that the path into the center of the labyrinth is the same as the path leaving the labyrinth —
into the center and back into the world — another
symbiotic and necessary relationship of dark and
light. Labyrinths help model these journeys: we
get home by going there and discovering at the
end of the circled journey that we have been there
all along.

As you walk the labyrinth today, be aware of the
angels singing. Listen to what they have to say to
you. Be prepared to accept the cosmic gift that is
waiting for you at home in the center.

Prayer

*Great and holy one, send your angels to guide
my path this day.*

WHAT IS HAPPENING!?!

Luke 2:8–20

In that region there were shepherds living in the fields, keeping watch over their flock by night. Then an angel of the Lord stood before them, and the glory of the Lord shone around them, and to them, "Do not be afraid; for see — I am bringing you good news of great joy for all people" to you is born this day in the city of David a Savior, who is the Messiah, the Lord. This will be a sign for you: you will find a child wrapped in bands of cloth and lying in a manger." And suddenly there was with the angel a multitude of the heavenly host, praising God and saying, "Glory to God in the highest heaven, and on earth peace among those whom he favors!" When the angels had left them and gone into heaven, the shepherds said to one another, "Let us go now to Bethlehem and see

this thing that has taken place, which the Lord has
made known to us."

Once when I was walking the labyrinth at Grace Cathedral in
San Francisco, I walked in awe at the diversity of the other
walkers. It was lunchtime, and people of every color in the
Crayola box of flesh-tone crayons were there, leaving their
shoes around the edge and reverently stepping gently onto
the labyrinth rug. Humanity, God's creative genius — some in
business attire, some in remnants of Haight-Ashbury, brown
hair, blond hair, purple and green hair, some with no hair at all,
tall people, short people, large people and small people, walking. Just walking. I thought how wonderful a world we would
live in if all of humanity could walk together in the world as
they are walking in the labyrinth — sometimes side by side,
sometimes coming together on the same path, sometimes on
different paths just walking in peace. Wouldn't it be terrific if
the walking behavior of humanity in the labyrinth in the aisle
of the church spilled over and was replicated on the labyrinth
of streets in the city?

A HOST OF SINGING ANGELS is a great advertis-
ing gimmick. But would you believe them any more
than you would believe a used car salesperson?
Would the shepherds notice the angels if they had
come in the daylight instead of the dark of night?

Wouldn't the shepherds be afraid at such a sight, even when the angels told them not to be afraid?

However frightened these shepherds were, they still started on their journey to their center to discover what was happening. What they discovered was love: pure uncontaminated love. Unconditional love! God's ultimate gift for humanity! The shepherds experienced what it was like to be loved and to love.

God's unconditional love was always there for the people; the people just didn't understand it. And God's love is always with us; we just forget about it sometimes. We look in all the wrong places for God. We look in all the wrong places for love and security.

Why is it that when little children are asked what part they want to play in the Christmas Eve pageant, each one invariably says, "I want to be a king." Even as young children, we are fascinated with power. That is not where God is. That is not where love is. That is not where security is. Looking with longing at the kings of the world, at the principalities and the powers, is the wrong way to look. God is in the stable, not the palace. God is in the manger, a homeless baby, a refugee.

Once a year we come like the magi in a Christmas Eve pageant, tripping over our robes. We come like the shepherds, whose head cloths keep slipping over our eyes. We come like the little angels, not remembering where to stand, and we gaze at a plastic doll, and we are reminded once again that all that is important in life is how well we love one another. Nothing is more important than that, not how we dress, not who our relatives are, not what kind of a house we live in, not how much money we have in our pockets or in the bank, not how many degrees we have, not what kind of a job we have. None of that matters. The only thing that really matters is how care-full-y, how full of care, we love one another. And that is what is happening! Today and every day, God is loving us unconditionally so that we may love one another.

What God is doing is of such significance that the entire cosmos reverberates with the signs. We need to be ready to see, and hear, and feel, and experience these signs of God-with-us.

As the angel said to the shepherds,

"Do not be afraid; for see — I am bringing you good news of great joy. . . . To you is born this day in the city of David a Savior, who is the Messiah, the

Lord. This will be a sign for you: you will find a child wrapped in bands of cloth and lying in a manger."

Prayer

I am not afraid. God goes before me always.

RECEIVING GIFTS

Matthew 2:1–12

... after Jesus was born in Bethlehem of Judea, wise men from the East came to Jerusalem, asking, "where is the child who has been born king of the Jews? For we observed his star at its rising, and have come to pay him homage." ... When they had heard the king, they set out; and there, ahead of them, went the star that they had seen at its rising, until it stopped over the place where the child was. When they saw that the star had stopped, they were overwhelmed with joy.... Then, opening their treasure chests, they offered him gifts of gold, frankincense, and myrrh. And having been warned in a dream not to return to Herod, they left for their own country by another road.

Aren't a maze and a labyrinth the same thing? This is a question often asked by those who have not had the experience of entering the heart of the labyrinth. One can get lost in a maze, winding up in dead ends and fearful of not being found. The path to the center of the labyrinth is clear and well-mapped with no danger of losing one's way. Each time I enter the sacred path and journey to the inner space, I know that I can focus on what I will find when I reach the center and what I will take with me when I make my way back into the world. Each time I make the pilgrimage, I find in the labyrinth, and in myself, a new way to look at my life. It provides me with an opportunity to recover some aspects of my spirit that I may have lost in my daily journey.

EVEN THOUGH JUST WALKING the labyrinth is a gift in itself, we are given another gift when we walk to the center of the labyrinth, our center, God's center. The gift may not be as tangible or as spectacular as gold, incense, or myrrh, but a gift nevertheless. Many experience the gift as an incredible sense of peace that seeps into the darkest and most hidden corners of our bodies, minds, and souls. Often, the gift comes as an insight or a thought, a revelation, or an incredibly deep understanding. Sometimes the gift is an answer to a question or solution to a perplexing problem. Once in a while, that which we receive is not recognized as a gift immediately, and it is only after some time has passed that what we received was the gift we needed. Oftentimes, that which we receive is something we didn't know or think we wanted, or may even be something we didn't want, but with time, the preciousness of the gift becomes clear.

While it is true that the gift of God's presence does not have to be in the center of a labyrinth — revelation comes to anyone who is ready and attuned to how the spirit works — praying the labyrinth is one way to prepare and tune ourselves to recognize the Spirit's gift when it arrives. The more we practice fine-tuning our inner sights to recognize the gifts the Spirit has for us, the more gifts we become aware of receiving. It's like having a gallbladder operation. Soon you begin to hear stories about gallbladder operations from your friends, from television, from the latest novel you are reading. There are so many operations you wonder why you hadn't heard about them before.

The more we accept the Spirit's gifts, the more we see the world around us as God's creation. The more we accept the riches of God's creation, the more we are able to let go of those things that block us from our relationship with God. The more we are able to let go of those things that block us from our relationship with God, the more we see the world around us as God's creation. A lovely spiral, a wonderful labyrinth that brings us closer and closer to God.

I find it very difficult at times to describe to people what a revelation or an encounter with God is like. The English language is woefully inadequate at this point. Others have tried to describe their experiences using metaphors of burning bushes, powerful dreams, angels singing, and stars shining more brightly than ever before. There are no words. There are no metaphors. But there is a knowing. When I was a child, my grandmother always had a little white bag of black licorice in the right-hand corner of the drawer of her desk. Whenever I visited, she always gave me a few pieces of licorice from that bag. The bag was always there, it always had licorice, and she always gave some to me. I knew she wouldn't let me down. I knew she wouldn't forget. She was always ready with her gift.

I know that when I walk the labyrinth, the Spirit's gift will be given to me. If one worries about whether the gift is there or not, it might be more difficult to recognize it. It's a matter of trust. It's about not fretting or worrying.

When you walk the labyrinth today, walk in excited anticipation knowing that you will be given a gift. Walk with your hands outstretched, open and palms up, ready to receive your unique and special gift. Do not worry. Do not try to second-guess the Holy Spirit. Humbly and with thankfulness, accept the gift. Know that God will not let you down. Know that God will not forget you.

Prayer

Just as I am, without one plea, I come, O Lord, I come.

I HAVE CALLED YOU BY NAME

Genesis 17
Luke 2:21

When Abram was ninety-nine years old, the LORD appeared to Abram, and said to him, "I am God Almighty; walk before me, and be blameless. . . ." God said to Abraham, "As for Sarah your wife, you shall not call her Sarai, but Sarah shall be her name. I will bless her, and moreover I will give you a son by her . . . and you shall name him Isaac." I will establish my covenant with him as an everlasting covenant for his offspring after him. . . .

After eight days had passed, it was time to circumcise the child; and he was called Jesus, the name given by the angel before he was conceived in the womb.

85

Maybe it was because the labyrinth was in a meadow, far from the noise of the city, far from the noise of my life. Maybe it was because I was alone in this field searching for the opening in the tall grasses that led to the labyrinth path and to the peace I was told would greet me when I eventually arrived at the center. Maybe it was because I couldn't see anyone else in any direction. Maybe it was because I could hear the insects buzzing and the gentle swish as the tall grasses brushed against each other. Whatever it was, I heard my name being whispered on the breeze, calling me to the center, guiding me around all the turnings and re-turnings of the labyrinth path. I began to sing softly to myself the words of a Celtic blessing, "May the road rise up before you, with the wind forever at your back. May the sun shine warm upon your face. May the rain fall soft upon your field. Until we meet again, may God hold you in the hollow of God's hand." By the time I entered the center of the labyrinth, I was being carried in God's hands. I was loved. I was called by name.

NAMING IS VERY IMPORTANT throughout the Bible stories. Many names have special meaning for the person and suggest how that person is to follow their spiritual path. Jesus' name was determined at conception, God with us. Often God changes a person's name to meet new circumstances. Abram and Sarai become Abraham and Sarah. When Jesus begins his ministry, he calls the disciples by name, and even changes Simon's name to Peter. The Holy Spirit changes Saul's name to Paul.

In some cultures and religious traditions, people have two names, the one by which they are known in the world and their spirit name, a name not known to many, if any, others. In the biblical stories, the re-naming is also a time of re-claiming and indicates a turning around, of being with God. Names offer identity.

When God changes Abram to Abraham and Sarai to Sarah, God is making a covenant with them. God writes the covenant into Abraham and Sarah's identity. God says: "I am God almighty; walk before me, and be blameless." From that point on, Abraham, Sarah, and God are walking together. God invites, or rather tells, Abraham and Sarah that they are to live out their lives in the very presence of God. God will not be distant, but ever-present. Abraham and Sarah obey. They go where God calls them to go. Sarah has a son and names him Isaac, which means laughter.

If God came to you right now and said, "I will be your God; walk before me and be blameless," what name would God give to you? What name would you like God to give you?

As you walk the labyrinth today, listen very carefully for your name. You may hear the name your parents chose for you. You may hear the name you chose for yourself. If you hear a different name, don't edit it. Just let it flow into your consciousness and remember what it is. When you have the opportunity, look up the name in a name book or on the Internet. If you believe that the name you received was your spirit name, keep it to yourself. Do not share it with anyone. Every time you walk the labyrinth, listen for your spirit name to be called, to lead you to the center. Hear God calling you: I have called you by name. You are mine. You are mine.

Prayer

Holy One, I hear you calling my name. Lead me, Lord.

Week Three

Walking the Path of Jesus

Jesus begins his ministry by calling people to follow him. Choosing to follow Jesus is a great deal more difficult than the writers of the Gospels describe. Jesus says to the fishermen, "Come, follow me." Immediately, they hop up and follow. They don't ask questions; they don't say good-bye to their friends and relatives. Simon Peter and Andrew leave their nets in a jumble, and James and John leave their father in the boat without any help. One has to wonder what was so compelling about this man Jesus that so many immediately chose to follow him without asking for his résumé or doing a background check. What was he offering to these people that so radiated from his presence that they were willing and ready to give up everything they already had to follow him?

After the calling of the disciples and for the next three years, Jesus and his friends walked and prayed, prayed and walked. Even though we can't walk around Galilee and Jerusalem in following

Jesus' footsteps very often, we can choose to follow Jesus and walk and pray with him wherever we are. Jesus is saying to you, "Come, follow me." "I am the way, the truth and the life. The way to have a transcendent experience or to know God is by following my example and my teachings. I know what I am talking about. Continue to do the kind of work I have been doing, and you will know God as I have known God."

Jesus was a master, one of the truly enlightened souls. He knew about transcendence, what it is like to experience God, and he wanted to share his experience with his friends and show them a way to transcendence. If you have chosen to be on the Christian path, then you have chosen to try to understand and live Jesus' teachings. You have chosen to try to walk the path that Jesus walked. You have chosen to trust that by living according to his way, you will experience God.

Jesus' path is like many paths braided into one. Jesus taught us about love, forgiveness, peace, healing, faithfulness, and thankfulness as well as justice, joy, and compassion. On some level, it is difficult to focus on one without including the others. For example, peace without justice is no peace. In order to forgive, one must have love in one's heart. What is also true is that if one forgives, one will experience love in one's heart.

When we start to walk any of these paths of Jesus, we begin to experience a "being" shift. It is not so much a changing of one's behavior as it is a changing of one's being. One's being starts to shift after days of practice and over a long period of time. Don't expect total transformation after one walk in the labyrinth. While I believe that this could happen, because with God all things are possible, I see transformation more like watching the tide come in. With every wave or walk or prayer, there is a gradual shift in our state of being.

"Disciple" and "discipline" are from the same root. To be a disciple means to have discipline, not in the sense of a fifth-grade teacher maintaining discipline in a classroom, but as a conscious choice to follow a spiritual practice. Walking a labyrinth every day is a spiritual practice. For Christians, the discipline is to follow Jesus on his path. The path of the labyrinth is a metaphor for the path that Jesus walked. As you walk the labyrinth this week, imagine that you are following Jesus, that you are walking the path Jesus walked.

Thomas Merton says that the "way to come into contact with the living God is to go to one's center and from there pass on to God." When we walk with Jesus to the center, we will come in contact with the living God and from the center we will pass on to God.

WALKING THE PATH OF LOVE

2 John 1:4–6

...But now, dear lady, I ask you, not as though I were writing you a new commandment, but one we have had from the beginning, let us love one another. And this is love that we walk according to his commandments; this is the commandment just as you have heard it from the beginning — you must walk in it.

The sense of walking into a holy space struck me as I entered the door of the great cathedral and soon encountered the labyrinth in the nave. I found it easy to ignore the distractions in this special place and to take the time I needed to relax as I prepared to start my journey into the labyrinth. As I entered the labyrinth, I chose the mantra that I have used on many other labyrinth walks since. "Let there be peace on earth and let it begin with me." The sense of walking alone and being at peace within myself was transcending. As I passed my daughter on a neighboring path, I was struck by the sense of peace I saw in her face. I was both alone and at peace in my mind and also connected in a profound loving way with my daughter.

WHAT IS THIS THING called love? For Christians, love is agape, a love that is spiritual, a love that has no ifs, ands, or buts about it. Sexual love is Eros. The love Jesus talks about is agape — to love unconditionally. We who are followers of Jesus have been given only one instruction. "This I command you, to love one another." Only one instruction and it sounds so very easy. But this may be the most difficult challenge in our lives. There is a small bit of good news in this command. Jesus never said that we have to like each other. On one hand, that is good news, but on the other, it may make following Jesus more difficult. It is very easy to love people we like. But that is not all that we have been called to do. Jesus doesn't say, "Love the people you like. Love the people with whom you get along well. Love the people who are just like you." The challenge for us, if we are to truly follow Jesus and to obey his command, is to love all of God's children, without exception, regardless of race, religion, nationality, sexual preference, age, class, gender, or behavior.

I imagine that most of us are able to say, in some general way, that we love, in the agape understanding of that word, all of God's children. But what about the person who pushes ahead of you in the check-out line at the supermarket when you are already late? What about people who are continuously antagonistic at meetings? What about parents who sexually abuse their children? What about teenagers who smash up the family car because they have been drinking? What about the Hitlers of the world?

How do we love the people that we do not like, or that drive us crazy, or that we believe in our heart of hearts are just plain wrong? Jesus commands us to love one another. And if we intend to be faithful followers of Jesus, we must constantly struggle with how to do that.

Jesus is the ultimate model of what it means to love absolutely and without question. Jesus said, according to John, "This is my commandment, that you love one another as I have loved you. No one has greater love than this, to lay down one's life for one's friends."

To lay down one's life in this context doesn't necessarily mean to physically die, but it does mean to die to your old way of thinking about or being with the other person. Christian agape love is not only a change of attitude; it is a whole new way of being. When Jesus engaged with others, there was no question that he loved them. The love Jesus radiated surrounded him like a very large aura. When one came close to him, one also felt surrounded by this incredible love. No wonder lives changed.

As you walk the labyrinth today, imagine that you are following Jesus close enough so that the unconditional love radiating from him encompasses you also. Feel the love surrounding you as you walk closer and closer to God.

Prayer

Gracious and Holy God, let me feel your love surrounding me this day and all my days.

WALKING THE PATH OF FORGIVENESS

Matthew 18:21–22

Then Peter came and said to him, "Lord, if another member of the church sins against me, how often should I forgive? As many as seven times?" Jesus said to him, "Not seven times, but, I tell you, seventy-seven times."

I had gone through life carrying a lot of pent-up anger over an incident when I was four years old. (I was molested by a neighbor.) I joined a church in 1999 that has a labyrinth. In learning about the labyrinth and its use as a prayer tool, I took my anger to the center with me one evening. I prayed to God to take this burden from me. Let me forgive this man and get on with my life. Well, I can't tell you how relieved I felt as I left the labyrinth that night. As the next few weeks went by, I was suddenly aware that my anger was gone. Walking the labyrinth every week, I continued to pray that this peace and calm would last. It has been six years now, and I continue to be a calmer and much happier person. God spoke to me that night.

TO TRULY EXPERIENCE FORGIVENESS, one also has to truly experience love. The converse is also true. To experience love, one also experiences forgiveness. While not necessarily two sides of a single coin, forgiveness and love are intertwined threads of a single cord.

Simon Peter asked Jesus a very difficult question, "Lord, if another member of the church sins against me, how often should I forgive? As many as seven times?" Jesus' response is overwhelming. What is really interesting about this passage is that Jesus is not addressing the person causing the pain, but he is telling those who have been hurt to forgive seventy times seven. This is a hard teaching. It is a difficult teaching because there are many situations when someone has hurt someone else, and the act is so heinous that it is difficult to think that the victim should ever forgive the perpetrator. However, what Jesus is saying is that it is necessary for us to forgive for the peace of our own soul. When we forgive someone, it is not for that person's sake, but for our own.

When we say, I'll never forgive that person for the hurt they have caused me, we think that our resentment is hurting the other person, when in fact, it is only devouring us. Throughout our lives, we get hurt, terrible things happen to us, and we hold on to resentments. These held resentments cause us to feel badly about ourselves and in turn cause us to behave in ways we may not want to behave.

This passage is not about "forgive and forget." It is also not saying that we should accept abuse from another. This passage suggests that we look at the resentment we are holding on to that is making us sick inside. This resentment may even make us perpetuate the same abuse that we have suffered onto another. Someone has to stop the pattern. Somehow we have to let the resentment go.

Our resentments are poisoning our own hearts, making us sick. We need to forgive for the peace of our own souls, but primarily, we forgive because God has already forgiven us.

The old saying "The only things for sure are death and taxes" is wrong. The only thing for sure is that God forgives us no matter what. God's love and mercy are boundless. We are God's children, and

God will never abandon us. Because we have experienced God's grace, we are enabled to forgive ourselves and others. Yet forgiveness may be the most difficult path for some of us to walk.

Today as you walk the labyrinth, think about someone from whom you have recently been estranged or with whom you are angry and with whom you would like to experience reconciliation. Try to hold an image of this person in your mind's eye and try to say, "[Person's name], I forgive you." This is agape. Try repeating this phrase over and over as you walk.

Prayer

Great and Gracious One, surround [person's name] and me with your holy reconciliation.

WALKING THE PATH OF PEACE

John 20:19–22

When it was evening on that day, the first day of the week, and the doors of the house where the disciples had met were locked... Jesus came and stood among them and said, "Peace be with you." After he said this, he showed them his hands and his side. Then the disciples rejoiced when they saw the Lord. Jesus said to them again, "Peace be with you. As the Father has sent me, so I send you." When he had said this, he breathed on them and said to them, "Receive the Holy Spirit."

Shoes, hundreds of shoes, spiraled into the center of the park on a chilly evening in September. Sandals, pumps, sneakers, boots, slippers, moccasins, oxfords, and clogs leading the way into the heart of the labyrinth and out again. Many of us had emerged from an interfaith church service commemorating the anniversary of September 11, 2001, and now we were trying to find some sense of peace in this ritual of mindfulness. The shoes had been donated for this occasion and would be sent to Iraq. As I set forth on my journey into the center, I wondered what I should be feeling. For the most part, I was paying attention to staying on the path and allowing enough room for those on their way back out of the spiral. Suddenly I was there! I felt a gathering of power from the people around me, a sense that we might find a way to act in the face of such sadness and anger. On my way back, I felt strengthened by the resolve of my companions and supported by the energy to continue with the ongoing work for peace.

JEREMIAH SAYS, "They have treated the wound of my people carelessly, saying, 'Peace, peace,' when there is no peace." Where is the peace? What does the word "peace" mean in our world and lives today? I watch TV, I read the papers, and I wonder where is the peace? Peace isn't just the opposite of a nation being at war, although that use of the word "peace" is certainly one tiny fraction of what I mean and what the Bible means. Peace is the opposite of violence of any kind. That includes violence in the form of sexual harassment, rape, and battering of women and children, and that includes how we treat each other in our work situations and in our families.

Peace isn't just the absence of violence either. Peace is a whole way of being and a whole new way of looking at the world. According to Paul, the path to salvation, as set forth in the life and teachings of Jesus, happens when all of the creatures in heaven and earth learn to play and sing and dance together in harmony. More than a feeling of oneness with God, more than a conviction that deep down we are all one with another, Christ's peace actually changes the relationship between people and brings us together in new ways. At the very least, Christ's peace is an attitude change, and at best, a behavioral change.

The language of Christianity is full of paradoxes. Rather than eliminating life's contradictions, Christianity asks us to struggle with them, to ponder their meaning and live in their tension, until they lead us to deeper understanding and increase our capacity for life and love. It is our choice, our individual choice and our collective choice, to choose peace over violence, to choose love over hate, and to choose life over death.

If you are walking the labyrinth today with many others, whether they be strangers or not, image in your mind's eye surrounding each fellow traveler with God's shalom. If you are walking alone, image the many people you have seen this day or week, whether stranger or not, and image in your mind's eye surrounding each of God's children with God's shalom of peace.

Prayer

Holy God, let there be peace on earth and let it begin with me.

WALKING THE PATH
OF HEALING

Mark 5:25–35

Now there was a woman who had been suffering from hemorrhages [issue of blood, KJV] for twelve years. She had endured much under many physicians, and had spent all that she had; and she was no better, but rather grew worse. She had heard about Jesus, and came up behind him in the crowd and touched his cloak, for she said, "If I but touch his clothes, I will be made well." Immediately her hemorrhage [issue of blood] stopped; and she felt in her body that she was healed of her disease. Immediately aware that power had gone forth from him, Jesus turned about in the crowd and said, "Who touched my clothes?" And his disciples said to him, "You see the crowd pressing in on you; how can you say, 'Who touched me?'" He looked all around to see who had done it. But the woman, knowing what had happened to her, came in fear and trembling, fell down before him, and told him the whole truth. He said to her, "Daughter, your faith has made you well; go in peace, and be healed of your disease."

I had a very hard decision to make. My husband could not get a job near the job I loved. Exasperating every effort I made to make a decision about what to do was the sheer pressure of time. The decision knotted up into a ball of string even a kitten could not unravel. This issue tied up with that issue which made a coalition with another issue. Feminism quarreled with family, then family with feminism. I was damned if I was going to be a woman who broke the stained-glass ceiling—and then give it up for family. I also couldn't do the job alone. I needed the support of my partner. I finally admitted that I had *no time* in which to pull the strings apart and see what I needed to do. I was also not keeping a regular Sabbath at that time. I was working all the time, rushing to save Miami from doing one stupid thing or another. Everything outside seemed to be more important than what was inside me — which was a growing confusion and fatigue.

What saved me was a walk in a labyrinth. I was so coiled up that I needed time to uncoil. I went to the woods in Kirkridge, a retreat center outside of Stroudsburg, Pennsylvania. I had been there many times — and even written a book about labyrinths from its centered peace. I needed to empty, to pour out, all the self-serving myths about my utter indispensability. After about four days of hiking around on the Appalachian Trail, in relatively desultory fashion, almost as though the back-and-forth were the pattern of my decision making paralysis, I fell into a deep sleep. I woke the next morning to all but rush out of the cabin around 6 a.m. I went straight to the labyrinth and said that I would walk in, and at the center, know which choice I was making. I would then walk out loving the choice I had made. To stay in Florida would have been fine. To leave Florida would also be fine. That was the message I gave myself on the way into the circle of circles the labyrinth was.

After these months of sickness-making indecision, I knew the time had come to decide. I had no idea what the decision would be. Instead I knew there would be a decision, that wonderful word that comes from *de cidere,* "to kill" as its root. I was going to kill one of the two possibilities for my life.

I got to the center of the labyrinth. There was a rock. I sat on it for what seemed a long time but what was actually a short time. The rock said, You are going back to Amherst. You are ending the commute. I said fine. I then walked out of the circle of circles, with a joy and lightness I can't remember. Something had died. Something was born. I had walked into it; now I was walking out of it.

I had taken a Sabbath in the circles. The Sabbath had given
me the rest to know what I should do. The labyrinth was just
the pattern of unraveling the yarns that had been all balled up.
The yarns were a messy version of the labyrinth. They mirrored
each other — one in its confusion, the other in its simplic-
ity. What made the difference? Why did this labyrinth break
through in decision on this day? Who knows? Because of this
trip to this labyrinth on this day, I walked out in peace. The
decision was made, and I thank the labyrinth for it.

THE WOMAN IN THE STORY from Mark has an issue
of blood. We all have issues. Some of our issues
make us physically ill. Some of our issues para-
lyze us from getting on with our lives, and we keep
stumbling over other issues in our lives. In this lesson, the woman is pro-active. She has come to a
time in her life when she says, "Enough is enough."
She reaches out and grabs onto Jesus' robes. There
was so much healing power emanating from Jesus
that just this one touch heals the woman instantly.
In many other of the healing stories of Jesus, Jesus
does the healing, but in this story, the woman takes
responsibility for her own healing. She chooses to
be healed. In the process, she does have to break
some of the taboos of her culture and time, such

as grabbing a man's robes. She risks being chastised by the disciples. She risks being crushed by the crowds. She risks being rejected by Jesus. But she knows, in her heart of hearts, that if she can just touch his robe, she will be healed. She reaches out, and as her hand touches the cloth, she feels the power of this holy man surge through her. Her issue no longer prevents her from living in wholeness. She no longer needs to bleed her life's energy away on her issue. She is now whole.

As you walk the labyrinth today, think about an issue that is preventing you from being whole, an issue that is bleeding away your energy. As you reach the center of the labyrinth, imagine reaching out and touching the robe of Jesus. Let his power surge through you. Be whole.

Prayer

Holy One, surround me today with your healing love. Let the power of this love so fill me that I also may reach out and touch someone and spread your healing through the world.

WALKING THE PATH
OF FAITHFULNESS

Luke 17:5–6

The apostles said to the Lord, "Increase our faith!"
The Lord replied, "If you had faith the size of a mustard seed, you could say to this mulberry tree, 'Be
uprooted and planted in the sea,' and it would obey
you...."

Entering the labyrinth is an act of faith for me. In other words
it is an unexpected practice for discovering the presence of
the Divine, which can and often does lead me to faithful action. I had a major decision pending, and this seemed like a
good way to clear out the underbrush of worries and focus
on the central concern. This particular moment was an unusual one. It was 3 a.m. in San Francisco, and I was walking

my "home" labyrinth at Grace Cathedral. For some long forgotten reason I was coming home from a visit with a friend at this early morning hour and realized that this prayerful walk could go a long way toward calming my inner voices so I could hear a more "centered" voice. So I bundled up and found myself all alone walking the outdoor seven-cycle labyrinth inspired by the Chartres Cathedral. I consciously allowed my walking to be a form of letting go of all thought and the thicket of worries that were pricking me so I could concentrate on my breath and my careful footsteps. By the time I had made it to the center I was quite clear about what I needed to do. My step was lighter as I walked back out of the center, and I could feel a smile growing. Again this simple practice had put me in a different space, a spiritual space where I could see and "hear" more clearly. I accepted gratefully the mysterious power of this simple walk of faith that also leads to faith.

THE APOSTLES ALWAYS STRUGGLE with the same issues and questions that we are constantly struggling with. I love the apostles. We often think of them as twelve holy and pious men. But truly they were a motley crew, asking impossible questions, like "Which one of us is the best disciple?" or wanting the quick cure for life issues like justice and faithfulness. Can't you just see the bunch of them hassling Jesus and saying, "Quick, Jesus, increase my faith." We would probably ask for the right pill or the best diet or something, "Quick, Jesus, I want to be faithful; just give me the right vitamin pill."

Imagine Jesus standing there with this gang, shaking his head and saying, "Oh no, where have I gone wrong?" Jesus, typical of his teaching style, doesn't give them the sure cure. He doesn't give them a book entitled *Seven Quick and Easy Sure-fire Methods to Increase Your Faith.* Instead, Jesus tells them a little story about weeds. Can you imagine such a thing? The people want their faith increased, and Jesus tells them about weeds. The mustard plant is a weed. Often we reflect on this story from the point of view of the size of the seed, thinking that somehow even the teeniest tiniest faith is all right. I think that is true, but the second half of the passage is even more enlightening.

"If you had faith the size of a mustard seed, you could say to this mulberry tree, 'Be uprooted and planted in the sea,' and it would obey you."

Maybe Jesus had more in mind than just a tiny seed faith. Why did Jesus tell the people to have faith like a weed rather than like a beautiful cultivated orchid or rose?

What can we learn from weeds and mustard seeds that will increase our faith and enable us to do those things that appear impossible at first glance? Certainly, on first appearance, it seems impossible for a tiny mustard seed to move a big mulberry tree.

In less than three weeks a vigorous mustard plant will produce more than four hundred feet of roots. A four-hundred-foot faith certainly seems different than a tiny seed's amount of faith.

Many of us view weeds as nuisances. One nuisance factor of weeds is that they compete with other plants, just as setting time for your spiritual practice competes with sleeping, reading the newspaper, having tea with a friend, or watching the kids' soccer practice.

Anyone who has a lawn has probably spent many hours trying to get the dandelions out. Most of us would consider dandelions as weeds. Many people spend many hours, dollars, and energy trying to rid their lives of this persistent weed. One day I spent time digging up little yellow dandelions so I could plant little yellow marigolds. I wondered what I was doing. Was the little yellow dandelion any less beautiful than the little yellow marigold? A dandelion is really quite beautiful, and a whole field of dandelions is spectacular and breathtaking.

The way dandelions spread their seeds is exceedingly clever, with those cute little fluffy parachutes that carry the seeds of faith and hope and deposit them right in the middle of the most pristine, sterile *Better Homes and Gardens* lawn. I have nothing against lawns per se, but imagine that the perfect lawn is a metaphor for our lives. Every blade of grass looks exactly like every other blade of grass, the same color, the same size, the same height, and the same age. As an ecosystem, lawns are boring; very few insects, birds, or animals can survive on a lawn as compared to a meadow or a field.

Then comes this little seed of faith that manages to plant itself in this sterile environment. It sends down an incredibly long root, taps the energy of the earth, and it blooms. This delicately beautiful flower courageously blooms right in the middle of all this mediocrity.

Jesus knew about weeds and seeds. He knew that even the tiniest seed of a weed could move the mulberry tree, and even the tiniest seed of faith could transform our ordinary lives into lives that are spectacular and breathtaking.

Weeds are tenacious, weeds are deeply rooted, weeds risk blooming where they are not wanted, weeds have remarkable powers of reproduction, weeds thrive under the worst conditions and the most incredible torture perpetrated on them by human beings, and weeds gathered together are spectacular and breathtaking. In every seed is the potential for new life, new green shoots, new flowers.

As you step onto the labyrinth path today, imagine planting a tiny seed. As you walk slowly to the center, imagine the seed bursting open, sending down a very long tap root, drawing in energy from the earth. Image your faith sprouting new green shoots. See the flower that you are, blooming as you reach the center.

Prayer

Creator God, let your love fall on me like gentle rain. Let your Son shine on me and fill me with energy so that I may grow in faith.

WALKING THE PATH OF THANKFULNESS

Colossians 3:12–17

Above all, clothe yourselves with love, which binds everything together in perfect harmony. And let the peace of Christ rule in your hearts, to which indeed you were called in the one body. And be thankful. Let the word of Christ dwell in you richly; teach and admonish one another in all wisdom; and with gratitude in your hearts sing psalms, hymns, and spiritual songs to God. And whatever you do, in word or deed, do everything in the name of the Lord Jesus, giving thanks to God. . . .

As I began my first labyrinth walk, I imaged giving over to the Holy Spirit all of my loved ones, so that I could make this

117

journey with a clear and uncluttered mind. I wondered if I were on the right path and remembered that there is only one path — one path that would take me to the center. My mind began to wander. What was I doing here? As I made one of the turnings I saw two quarters on the path. Bending, I quickly picked them up, thinking that someone must have dropped them. As I reached the center, I began to see more and more coins. The quarters had been an offering, left by a fellow walker. Amused at myself, I placed the quarters with the others along with my own offering. My mind started running, Did I leave enough? What is enough? Will I ever have enough? Enough time? Enough food? Enough money? Enough energy? Enough rest? Enough joy? I've had more than enough suffering. Just as I thought that my mind wouldn't stop screaming about enough, I started on my outward journey. I felt the breath of God moving around me and within me. On the breath, I heard the answer, "You are on the right path. You got here by following the path and letting it unfold. There is more than enough to go around, and you will have enough."

ON THE AVERAGE, how many times a day do you really give thanks to God, excluding grace at meals? We use the "thank you" phrase so often that it has lost its real meaning. "Thank you for the nice present." "Thank you for holding the door." "Thank you for sending over the casserole." The words just naturally tumble out. We say "Thank you" because we were trained as young children to say "Thank you," not necessarily because we really mean it or because we really understand it. It has become a habit without meaning.

In the Bible, thanksgiving is far from trivial. It is the number-one way we are to be in the world and with God. Thanksgiving is how we are to live, not a day to eat too much turkey and pumpkin pie. Thanksgiving, giving thanks, is more than being polite. Politeness has nothing to do with it; turkey has nothing to do with it. Walking in a state of thankfulness is how we are to walk, not just in the labyrinth today, but every day of our lives.

Walking in thankfulness is to walk in gratitude. It is to live our lives in a state of a very constant and very enthusiastic, "Thank you, God." We forget sometimes, maybe most of the time, that we already have everything that we need to be happy, not a surface happy, but a real deep-down-in-the-soul happy, because happiness comes from inside us. If we believe that happiness comes to us from others, we will be disappointed too many times. When we start to believe that true happiness comes from within our own centers, from the God-within-us, the happiness leaks out, turns into deep gratitude, and we begin to walk in a life-changing thankfulness.

As you walk the labyrinth today, think of all of the things for which you are thankful. After each one, say, "Thank you."

Prayer

Thank you, God.

WALKING THE PATH OF W-HOLINESS

2 Corinthians 7:1

Since we have these promises, beloved, let us cleanse
ourselves from every defilement of body and of spirit,
making holiness perfect in the fear of God.

The first time I walked a labyrinth and made the first turn, I
nearly dropped my teeth—and they are not false. It was a jaw-
dropping experience that shot through my whole being. I was
screaming, "Yes!" inside myself as the outer power of turning
and returning, of walking closer and further away clicked together with all those inner life experiences that had felt the
same way. My inner landscape felt enormous relief in having an external way of making memories of choosing this, not
that, palpable. These building blocks of my life now became

outer companions that could be met, embraced, and honored. Luckily, I was alone in the labyrinth because it became fully inhabited with life experiences that I walked with and through and that I ultimately released into the center. On the way into the center, each turning evoked more and more of my inner landscape. At the center, I offered this fullness of self — the good, the bad, and the beautiful — as gift. On the way out, each turning brought a bon voyage and a "Godspeed" to these pieces of my past. As I stepped out of the labyrinth and back into time and place, I felt cleansed, purified, enlightened, and present to myself from the top of my head down to the soles of my feet.

IN HIS POEM "A Psalm for the Feast of Autumn," Edward Hays says: "In sacred dance, great hosts of brown leaves circle-turn before earth's altar, whirling round like brown-robed Sufis, lost in the ecstasy of God."

For many of us, before we are able to let go and get lost in the ecstasy of God and before we can truly walk in pure w-holiness, we must purify ourselves from everything that contaminates the body and spirit; we have to unlearn some of our training. Most importantly, we have to let go of dualistic thinking. When we think in a dualistic way, we tend to create opposites and then set the opposites in a cosmic struggle, such as putting people in groups because of the color of their skin — black or white. But people aren't black or white, they are every color of the God's earth-tone colors. Have you ever seen a box of Crayola crayon flesh tones? There is no black or white!

The number of dualistic opposites we have arbitrarily constructed is legion. Good must overcome evil. Light must overcome dark. We tend to align ourselves with the "us" and designate "them" as the enemy. Dualistic thinking then justifies behaviors that lead us into hatred and war, not love and peace and certainly not to wholeness and holiness.

Artificial distinctions and categories keep us out of touch with what God wants for us, which is wholeness. Unfortunately, they are built into our very vocabulary and language. We need to practice new ways of talking and walking. We need to be thinking in inclusive ways and not in ways that try to exclude. The yin-yang symbol of Eastern religions might help. Rather than being viewed as opposites, the yin and yang are complementary, working together toward wholeness, not in a tug-of-war that constantly pulls us off our path to wholeness.

We carry around a great deal of unnecessary baggage — held resentments, paranoid fantasies, dualistic thinking, shoulds, oughts, and if onlys. To get lost in the ecstasy of God, we have to unburden ourselves. We have to let these thoughts and behaviors go. Jesus says, "Come to me, all you that are weary and are carrying heavy burdens, and I will give you rest." Do not be afraid to let some of these burdens go. We have a choice about what we carry around with us. We can travel heavy or we can travel light. We can carry every big hurt and every little hurt that has ever happened to us or that we have inflicted on others. Today is the day to sort through some of our baggage. This is the day to lay some of your burden down.

Today as you walk the labyrinth, metaphorically carry your burden to the center of the labyrinth and lay it down. The more you let go of, the more whole/holy you will feel. The lighter you will feel. Allow the light-ness to surround and fill you. Feel the Holy Spirit lift you up like a bird in flight. Let your light-ness spread out around you, bringing peace, hope, joy, healing, and love to everyone you meet.

Prayer

Today, O God, I lay at your altar [insert name of your burden], which I have been carrying by myself for so long.

Week Four

Transcendence

The thing about holy moments or transcendent glimpses is the more you have them, the more you have them, and the more you want them. It isn't true that we are blessed with only one or two epiphany experiences per lifetime. These moments are around us all the time. We only have to have ears to hear and eyes to see, and I would add a lot of letting go — a letting go of expectations.

Transcendent moments are only that. A brief moment in time, but a moment in time that changes one's life. People throughout the ages have tried to express in words what these holy moments are like. The best we can do is talk in metaphors. Martin Luther King in his famous speech said, "I have been to the mountaintop, I have seen the promised land." There is no doubt that Martin Luther King experienced a transcendent glimpse of God.

These holy moments happen anywhere and everywhere. They are glimpses into heaven. They don't make any logical sense. For the most part, they cannot be planned for, but they can be prepared for. Most of all, they can be expected. I have experienced many holy moments, and I know I will experience more. It's like not worrying about whether the sun will rise. It will! The only difference between the sun rising and transcendent experiences is that transcendent experiences happen at any time of the day or night and almost always as surprises.

Several years ago, I had pneumonia and was quite sick, unable to get out of bed. My close-in women friends, all members of the same church I attended, decided enough was enough. They gathered around my bed for a hands-on healing prayer. At the time, I was more than skeptical about healing prayer, but I was in no condition to complain or argue. During the prayer, in my mind's eye, but vivid enough that it felt like I was watching a movie on a screen, I saw several large butterflies. They had surrounded the dis-ease in my lungs with barely perceptible threads. The butterflies started to fly up toward the ceiling, pulling the pneumonia out of me. I was healed, but more importantly, I was transformed.

But that wasn't all of the story. When my friends left, I literally popped out of bed, went to the piano, and wrote a song, words and music, just like that. I had never written a song before in my life! The words of the song that floated on my internal viewing screen were the words of the prophet Micah.

> With what shall I come before the Lord?
> With what shall I worship God?
> Offerings of gold?
> Rivers of oil?
> My children or my toil?
> What is it that God wants of me?
> To do justice, to love kindness,
> And walk with my God in humility!

I have written many songs since that moment, and for the most part they just pop onto my screen and I write them down.

Because I have experienced so many of these holy moments, I can trust that I will have more. In my early days as a preacher, I used to be anxious every week about whether I would be able to write or preach another sermon. Once I let go of the worry and trusted the process, each week's sermon came to me just as regularly as the rising sun. I still am in awe about how that happened. I can't explain it; I can only try to describe it. One time, I woke up at about four o'clock in the morning. I went to my computer. Barely awake, I typed in the whole sermon and then went back to bed. The next morning, I read what I had written. What astonished me and astonishes me still is that I didn't even have to change a word, a period, or a comma. I kept asking myself, Did I write this?

Was this a transcendent moment? According to my secular dictionary, transcendent has to do with being "beyond" explanation or perception. I believe that my transcendent experiences or holy moments are those times when there is a crack in the wall that separates me from God. I believe that in these instances, the Holy Spirit slips through into my life in clear ways that I can perceive. But the "beyond perception" is no longer beyond; it is a real, albeit indescribable, present/presence to me. I only have to have eyes to see, ears to hear, and senses to feel.

As I suggested in Week Two, there is always a gift for us when we walk to the center of the labyrinth. When you walk this week, be prepared, watch, listen, allow the Holy Spirit to slip through the cracks in the wall you have built to separate yourself from God's self. Be in awe and be thankful. The holy moment, the gift of the Spirit, is waiting for you.

WAITING, WATCHING, WONDERING

Mark 13:32–37

"But about that day or hour no one knows, neither the angels in heaven, nor the Son, but only the Father. Beware, keep alert, for you do not know when the time will come. It is like a man going on a journey, when he leaves home and puts his slaves in charge, each with his work, and commands the doorkeeper to be on the watch. Therefore, keep awake — for you do not know when the master of the house will come, in the evening, or at midnight, or at cockcrow, or at dawn, or else he may find you asleep when he comes suddenly. And what I say to you I say to all: Keep awake."

In early May of 2006 I had been on my conscious spiritual journey for exactly thirty years. In that time my understanding of what constitutes a miracle expanded and deepened. But a very clear miracle happened one day when I was walking the labyrinth at Grace Cathedral. I felt my mortality, and in that feeling was the presence of the Divine. Allow me to explain. Usually we don't watch our feet when we walk (at least I certainly don't). But that day I was watching my feet, feeling the movement of my heels and toes as I deliberately tried to stay on the narrow path of the labyrinth. (Even that it was a narrow path seemed significant that day.) As I was doing that I had this overpowering sense that I was alive, that I was a unique person, and then the more profound truth struck me. The Spirit of God somehow (and I don't know how) lived in my body. And my body was connected to the earth and to a spiritual path — the cycles of the labyrinth — through the touch and movement of my feet. I had to stop, take a deep breath, and then walk the narrow path to the center and out again with this almost incomprehensible mystery buzzing through my body. All I know is that it is a miracle and a mystery that the Spirit of God lives within human bodies. In my body! That was enough for one day.

WE'VE FORGOTTEN how to identify miracles. Oftentimes we miss the opportunity to be the angel in someone else's miracles. Because of our school-ing and training in this computer age, we have lost our natural ability to identify a miracle when it is happening, often attributing the whole thing to coincidence. Many of us are afraid to share our mir-acle stories for fear of being labeled crazy. Mostly, we no longer even expect miracles.

Being a watcher of miracles requires no special degrees and no special training, but there are some requirements and some assumptions.

The first requirement is believing that miracles happen. We've lost our sense of expectation. We just don't expect God to do much in and through our lives. But if we have faith, and if we would allow the possibility, we will begin to recognize all that God is doing for us and through us. Our basic prob-lem is not that we expect too much from God, but that we do not expect anything.

There is something that we can learn from chil-dren, and that is how to wait with eager anticipa-tion. We tell ourselves that we are too old to stand on tippy toes, watching, waiting, and wondering what miracle God is going to do next. Every day of our lives, we should ask the question as we get out of bed in the morning, "I wonder what the Holy Spirit is going to do today."

The second requirement is that we have to watch for the coming Christ, not necessarily in some cosmic fireworks display, but in the people and events of everyday life. I haven't figured out yet whether our basic problem is that we don't know *how* to look for miracles or that we don't know *where* to look for miracles. I do know that because we have been so well trained in being rational human beings, and because we live in a society that is strongly influenced by science, we have a tendency to write miracles off as coincidence. I would encourage you to begin to consider the coincidences in your lives and in the lives of those around you from the point of view of the intervention of the Holy Spirit, from the point of view of a miracle.

The third requirement is that we open ourselves up to be used by the Holy Spirit in the bringing about of miracles. Sometimes, actually most of the time, it is very difficult to determine how we are being used until after the miracle has been identified. But if we want to be used by the Holy Spirit in miracle making, we have to open ourselves up to that possibility and be willing to trust the still small voice inside of us.

As you walk the labyrinth today and every day, ask yourself, "I wonder what the Holy Spirit is going to do today." Start watching for the miracles. And when you go to bed at night, thank God for the miracles you were a part of or the miracles that you watched.

Prayer

Holy Spirit, awaken me to your presence in my life.

ON THE ROAD AGAIN

Luke 24:13–35

Now on that same day two of them were going to a village called Emmaus, . . . and talking with each other about all these things that had happened. While they were talking and discussing, Jesus himself came near and went with them, but their eyes were kept from recognizing him. And he said to them, "What are you discussing with each other while you walk along?" They stood still, looking sad. Then one of them, whose name was Cleopas, answered him, "Are you the only stranger in Jerusalem who does not know the things that have taken place there in these days?" He asked them, "What things?" They replied, "The things about Jesus of Nazareth, who was a prophet mighty in deed and word before God and all the people, and how our chief priests and leaders handed him over to be condemned to death and crucified him. But we had hoped that he was the one to redeem Israel. Yes, and besides all this, it is now the third day since these things took place. Moreover, some women of our group astounded us. They were at the tomb early this morning, and when they did not find his body there, they came back and told us that they had indeed seen a vision of angels who said that he was alive. Some of those who were with us went to the tomb and found it just as the women had said; but they did not see him. . . . " As they came near the village to which they were going, he walked ahead as if he were going on. But they urged him strongly, saying, "Stay with us, because it is almost evening and the day is now nearly over." So he went in to stay with them. When he was at the table with them, he took bread, blessed and broke it, and gave it to them. Then their eyes were opened, and they recognized him; and he vanished from their sight. They said to each other, "Were not our hearts burning within us while he was talking to us on the road, while he was opening the scriptures to us?" . . . They were saying, "The Lord has risen indeed, and he has appeared to Simon!" Then they told what had happened on the road, and how he had been made known to them in the breaking of the bread.

I was co-teaching a seminar on writing and spirituality. We had approximately thirty attendees, and we were at a lovely retreat center in the high mesa of New Mexico. One of the events scheduled by my teaching colleagues was a labyrinth walk. A beautiful labyrinth had been set up with candles in bags along the path. For some of the attendees this was a first experience of walking the labyrinth, and they were pleasantly surprised by the subtle but powerful effect of doing this simple spiritual practice. At one point I took a few minutes to walk the path myself, although I was preoccupied with rearranging some of the content of my presentation. But as I walked the simple path it began to dawn on me slowly that this was a remarkable adventure of journeying with these young and old writers. I wasn't just teaching; I was on a journey toward God with them, in this place and at this time. Fortunately I was not the major speaker, and I could relax a bit and allow our leader to take us all on this journey together, which she did gently but firmly. I walked out of the labyrinth grateful for the grace-filled opportunity to see this retreat from a new perspective and also grateful for the consistent way that walking the labyrinth helps me see my own spiritual life more clearly.

IN THIS STORY, Christ comes to the two travelers on the road. Many of the stories of Jesus' life take place on the road. One of the curious parts in this story is that these two people did not recognize the Christ while they were on the road. One reason they may not have recognized Jesus was that they were too intent on rehashing all the terrible things that were happening. They were caught up in the negative energy, the negative feelings of the events.

The two people wanted to keep the churned-up feelings churned up. They didn't want to believe what God had done. They chose not to believe the women who had seen a vision of angels and had told the group that Jesus was alive. Sometimes we too want to keep the negative feelings churned up and not believe what God has done and continues to do.

Another reason that the two did not recognize Jesus on the road was that they may have been going in the wrong direction. They were heading away from Jerusalem. They were walking away from it all.

In terms of our spiritual journeys, the image of the road provides us with endless possibilities for glimpses into ourselves and our lives, our relationships with others, and our relationship with God. For example, is your road filled with potholes? Are you constantly falling into holes or pits? Some of us are afraid to go down those pothole-filled roads because we are afraid of falling into one of those pits and never being able to get out. For some of us, being on a spiritual journey may mean going down the road with the potholes and tending and caring for what is in the holes. The way to God and wholeness is to begin to care and nurture ourselves, especially the parts of us that are hurting. When we love ourselves, we can change the *hole* into *whole* and then into *holy.*

Some of us on spiritual journeys have experienced detours or dead ends. We think we know where we are going, only to find that we have come to a dead end, like in a maze. We feel dead inside. Nothing matters anymore. The road we have chosen may be alcohol or drugs, food or TV. It may be thinking that work is our salvation. It may be in believing that we are not *whole* unless we have a partner. There are a myriad of dead-end roads. The roads of money, prestige, and power often become dead ends, or may make us feel dead inside.

Sometimes we take detours. Detours aren't necessarily bad. On detours you end up going somewhere that you hadn't expected to go. You may discover something that you didn't even know you needed to discover.

Some of us are afraid to venture into the intersections in our lives because we are not sure which road to take next.

Then there are the roads that are very familiar. The roads where you know everyone, where you know every turn and bump, where you don't have to think, just go. Some of us live the same way, day in and day out, staying on the same path, never changing our patterns. We never get a map out to see if there might be another way, a way that may be unfamiliar, but a new way that may be just as pleasant once we get used to it, a new way that may offer something to us that we didn't even know we were missing.

And some of us go through our lives as if we were perpetually on a superhighway. Five lanes of traffic going at incredible speed! One of the problems with being in the fast lane is that it is easy to miss the rest stops.

In this story from Luke, there is a rest stop. Jesus and the two travelers go home for a meal. And it is in the breaking of the bread that they finally recognize Jesus. In our story, the people were on the road to Emmaus, but after they experienced Jesus at home, they were ready to go on the road again.

This time, however, they turned around and went back to Jerusalem.

The journey never ends, but it may change direction. You may find yourself going down roads you never thought you would go down. This story is about change and transformation. It is about the change that comes about because we encounter Jesus on the road. When the people recognized Christ, they stopped what they thought they were going to do, turned around, and went out on the road again.

As you walk the labyrinth today, pay attention to the road you are on and let it go. Let it change into the labyrinth path that will take you to the center of your being. Let the labyrinth path be your path to God.

Prayer

Holy One, guide me to your path.

EYE OF
THE STORM

Mark 4:35–41

On that day, when evening had come, he said to them, "Let us go across to the other side." And leaving the crowd behind, they took him with them in the boat, just as he was. Other boats were with him. A great windstorm arose, and the waves beat into the boat, so that the boat was already being swamped. But he was in the stern, asleep on the cushion; and they woke him up and said to him, "Teacher, do you not care that we are perishing?" He woke up and rebuked the wind, and said to the sea, "Peace! Be still!" Then the wind ceased, and there was a dead calm. He said to them, "Why are you afraid? Have you still no faith?" . . .

I decided to walk the labyrinth, even though the weather looked threatening and it was getting late in the day. I tend to be a fair-weather kind of labyrinth walker, and I usually walk in the early mornings. The fog was coming in off the bay, and all I could see with any clarity was the front of the church (the labyrinth is on the front patio) and some of the markings for the path. I continued to walk, wondering what I was doing in this place at this time and in this weather. But the labyrinth had its way with me. My surroundings seemed to disappear. As I approached the center, I was calmer and more at peace than I had ever been before. There was a warmth that I couldn't explain. It was almost as if I were glowing.

ONE OF THE CURIOUS THINGS about hurricanes is that at the center is an incredible calm. All that fury swirling around a beautiful peace! One of Jesus' and one of God's favorite phrases is "Do not be afraid." Jesus adds this time, "Why are you afraid? Have you still no faith?" The disciples are terribly anxious, because the winds swirling around them appear to be about to drown them. The disciples are no different than we are. The more anxious we are, the more anxious we get. We all have storms or potential storms swirling around us. But we also have choice. We can allow the storms of our lives to upset our boats so we drown, or we can have faith and find the calm that exists in the center.

I find it somewhat curious that the meteorologists call the calm center of a storm the eye. I realize that from space the center of a hurricane does look like an eye, but could it also be that in the center, in the calm, peaceful center, we see things differently? Is it possible that when we find our center, we see with different eyes? Our perspective changes, and we are blessed with in-sight.

There is a hard lesson to be learned from hurricanes. Hurricanes are necessary for the balance of energy on the planet. We only see great storms as forms of destruction, but in fact, hurricanes are like giant freight trains, moving energy from the equator to the poles. Being in a hurricane, whether it is a real hurricane or a metaphorical one, is not pleasant. But the winds of life, the winds of change, the winds of a great hurricane are necessary for balance, are necessary for life. It's not the hurricane or the storms in your life that are the trouble, but how you deal with them that makes a difference.

Remember that the disciples panic. Panic is one of our choices. But there are other choices. The disciples also call on Jesus to do something. That is also one of our choices. Jesus says to the winds, "Quiet, be still." Jesus is not only saying this to the storm, but he is saying this also to the storms of fear and anxiety that live within each of us. "Be still." Another choice! We can choose to stay in the stormy winds of fear and anxiety, or we can choose to be still. Jesus asks, "Why are you afraid?" We can ask ourselves the same question. "Why am I afraid?" "What am I afraid of?" Another choice! We can choose to be afraid, or we can choose not to be afraid. When the storms of life are raging, ask yourself, "What am I afraid of?"

Another curiosity about hurricanes is that the winds blow from one direction at the beginning, then there is calm, then they blow from the other direction. It is difficult to know where to stand, sometimes, with events changing around you so quickly and with such vehemence. It is so easy to get caught up in the winds of the storm that we forget that the storm comes designed with its own calm center, a place of sunshine and blue sky. This is the place to be — in the eye of the storm, in the place of calm. Here there is no need to be afraid.

As you walk the labyrinth today, imagine one of the storms in your life swirling around you. Hear Jesus say to you, "Why are you so afraid? Quiet!

Be still." As you walk toward the center of the labyrinth, know that you will find peace and calm at the
center.

Prayer

*When the storms of life surround me, stand
by me.*

LOST AND FOUND

Luke 15:4–10

... "Or what woman having ten silver coins, if she loses one of them, does not light a lamp, sweep the house, and search carefully until she finds it? When she has found it, she calls together her friends and neighbors, saying, 'Rejoice with me for I have found the coin that I had lost.' Just so I tell you, there is joy in the presence of the angels of God over one sinner who repents."

My sister and I decided to spend the day checking out some of the many labyrinths in the suburbs of Chicago. We had our maps, we had our directions, and off we went. The first labyrinth was a beautiful stone path in a peaceful backyard of an Episcopal Church. We visited a few others. As the day now was getting late, we decided to search for one more before we went

home. We had good directions. We were even able to find a
place to park. The directions said the labyrinth was part of
the Riverside Park. We walked up and down the riverbank. We
searched high and low. Where was it? We gave up and decided
to go and have a latte. Before we left where we were searching,
we went to read a plaque that was near where we were standing. It said, "This labyrinth in memorial of. . . . " We looked down
at our feet. We were standing in the labyrinth. The late afternoon sun had caught the edges of the stones in such a way that
we couldn't see the labyrinth, even though we were standing
right in it.

IT SEEMS SOMETIMES that half of everything I own
is lost. I never can find my keys. I'm always searching for my glasses. As I age, the problem seems to
increase exponentially. There are some things I'd
love to lose. Like pounds, for example! The woman
in the story lost a coin. Her response to finding it
was one of jubilation. "Rejoice with me!" she cries.
So is the losing or finding what's important here?
Losing things and finding things doesn't warrant
such joy. I think we might be better off if we didn't
have such emotional attachments to things. Jesus
says, "Sell all that you own and distribute the money
to the poor, and you will have treasure in heaven;
then come, follow me." Jesus certainly didn't have

attachments to things and the detritus of living. So what can this story mean for us? What does the coin represent to you?

The story could be referring to losing a part of ourselves, pounds notwithstanding. We lose a part of ourselves when we participate in activities that do not bring joy to our lives. We lose parts of ourselves when we allow ourselves to be sucked dry by family or work. It is so painful and yet so easy to lose oneself in an abusive relationship.

Often we are so busy losing ourselves in our work that we don't take the time to find ourselves, to find our holy centers. My life gets so frantic at times that I don't have time to meditate. When I don't take time to meditate, pray, and reflect on my life experience, I lose part of myself. I become shrew-like and even hostile.

While I probably would be glad at finding some thing I had lost, the joy would be nothing compared to finding a part of my self that was lost. I would indeed want to shout, "Rejoice with me; I have found what I had lost."

I'm always losing the keys to my car. But maybe what is really lost is the key to wholeness and holiness, the key to centeredness and inner peace. The woman in the story looks everywhere. She sweeps in the darkest corners of her home. We also have to be brave enough to look in the darkest corners for the key to our wholeness and holy-ness.

When I clean house, I usually make a bigger mess than I started with in order to sort things into piles: throw-out-now, throw-out-sometime, or keep-forever piles. Maybe we have to tear our lives totally apart and sweep in every dark corner to find the key to our self and to find God.

Maybe we metaphorically have to let ourselves fall to pieces, so that we can re-sort ourselves into piles: throw out now, throw out sometime, or keep forever. In the re-sorting, we may even find some parts of ourselves that we had lost or had forgotten we had. When we've sorted out ourselves/piles, we can reassemble ourselves. Then we can shout with joy, "Rejoice with me; I have found what I had lost." "So I tell you," Jesus says, "there is joy in the presence of the angels of God over one who repents."

Today, imagine that at each turning of the labyrinth there is a dark corner where the key to your life lies hidden.

Prayer

Holy Spirit, guide my search this day. Shine light into all of the dark corners of my life.

FROM STRESS TO STRENGTH

2 Corinthians 4:16–18

So we do not lose heart. Even though our outer nature is wasting away, our inner nature is being renewed day by day. For this slight momentary affliction is preparing us for an eternal weight of glory beyond all measure, because we look not at what can be seen but at what cannot be seen; for what can be seen is temporary, but what cannot be seen is eternal.

At a labyrinth retreat I led recently, we, of course, ended the retreat with a labyrinth walk. For this particular walk, as the priest, I shared communion/Eucharist with each journeyer as he or she approached the center of the labyrinth. There was something so spiritually different and so profoundly moving about this experience for me that I still choke up when I think about it. There certainly are no words that come close to describing the feeling I had. Each pilgrim had taken a long journey to arrive at the center. They had taken a long time to get there. This wasn't a pro-forma act of piling into the aisles and hurrying on so everyone could get home for Sunday lunch. Each person came to the table with a spiritual intention and a deep peace in their souls. As I looked into each participant's eyes, I knew that they too were experiencing God's grace, which passes all understanding.

PAUL WRITES, "Even though our outer nature is wasting away, our inner nature is being renewed day by day." If Paul were here today, he probably would have said, "Daily living is taking its toll — physically, emotionally, and mentally — on living our lives in a holy way." Paul says twice in this chapter that we should never become discouraged. Even though our physical bodies may be decaying, our spiritual bodies are being renewed day after day. So although we find ourselves in stressful life situations, we can change the stress to strength.

Paul doesn't mean that we should find ways to suffer so we will have eternal glory. He doesn't mean, "Suffering is good for you." What he means is, "Suffering happens." "Pain happens." Paul is trying to tell us that when we find ourselves in these painful places, or when we feel as if we are suffering, we still will receive the gift of God's love and grace.

How can we grow into our strength when life is providing us with all too many stressful situations? How can we make choices that will change stress into strength instead of into cancer, high blood pressure, strokes, and heart attacks?

A few possibilities. First of all, we have to live in hope. Paul was looking toward those things as yet unseen, but still anticipated. This hope kept him from losing heart. Believe in the future, but don't worry about the future. Jesus said, "So do not worry about tomorrow, for tomorrow will bring worries of its own. Today's trouble is enough for today."

Most stress comes about because we are human beings who are in relationships with other human beings, and when more than two human beings are gathered there is bound to be conflict. Conflict happens. Conflict happens because we are human beings, with different values, different expectations, different goals, different dreams, different fears, different life experiences, and different story lines.

What we forget is that conflict can be creative. Conflict can be a time for growth. And most assuredly, conflict provides us with opportunities to go from stress to strength.

Another way to change stress to strength is to begin to look at how we deal with conflict. The old saying that there are only two ways to deal with conflict, fight or flight, is wrong. There are alternatives. If people are to be in healthy relationships, and if people are to begin to change stress into strength, we have to start by sharing our stories with each other. Instead of fighting with each other, or instead of running away from each other, we need to share our stories with each other. I don't mean just surface sharing either. I mean deep-down-in-the-guts sharing. Instead of making assumptions about what other people feel, think, hope, and fear, we need to share what we feel, think, hope, and fear and let the others do the same. I know we would be surprised.

We need to sit down and check out the assumptions that are being made. We need to share our hopes and fears and to try to identify what the conflict is really about and then together design a resolution that takes the needs of everyone into consideration. There are many more ways of dealing with conflict than fighting or running away. When people creatively use conflict, it becomes a source of incredible strength and growth.

In changing stress into strength, we must remember to trust in God. I know that saying, "Don't
worry, trust God." can sound very trite and has almost become a cliché. But I happen to be very
serious.

One of the mistakes I make and maybe you make
is that I want God to do things my way. I want God
to do what I want. To trust in God is not to assume
that God will do things my way. That is not trusting
in God.

Trusting in God means that I do what God wants.
It means that I do things God's way. Everyone
knows what God wants of us. It is no secret. God
wants us to live our lives in God's way, and God's
way is the way of love, forgiveness, and compassion. To trust in God means to forgive people who
have hurt you. That does not mean you have to like
them or like what they did. It also does not mean
that you have to stay in relationship with them. It
does mean letting go of whatever it is that is hurting
you and causing you stress.

As you walk the labyrinth today, metaphorically
leave beside the path all of the different stresses
of your life. Gather your strength in the center of
the labyrinth. As you walk out of the labyrinth, pick
up one or two of the stresses you placed on your

way in. You don't have to pick them all up. Imagine holding this stress compassionately. Allow it to bring you strength.

Prayer

Holy Spirit, shower me with discernment so that I may be able to cross the bridge from stress to strength, pain to gift, and sorrow to joy.

JOURNEY
TO WHOLENESS

John 5:5–8

One man was there who had been ill for thirty-eight years. When Jesus saw him lying there and knew that he had been there a long time, he said to him, "Do you want to be made well?" The sick man answered him, "Sir, I have no one to put me into the pool when the water is stirred up; and while I am making my way, someone else steps down ahead of me." Jesus said to him, "Stand up, take your mat and walk."

The idea of walking a labyrinth was immediately appealing to me. I absolutely love to walk, and I absolutely love to meditate! These are two things that can almost always be counted on to save me from anxiety, self-doubt, sluggishness, and despair.

Sometimes when I am out walking, I slow way down and begin a walking meditation. Now here was a beautiful structure, the labyrinth, in which to walk and meditate, and no one would think it odd. My only question was, What would it be like to walk in a labyrinth with other people? Would it be distracting? Would I bump into other people?

When I got the chance to walk a labyrinth, I loved it. It was wonderful to be in the same space with others who were also walking with a spiritual purpose. It had the same power as group meditation, the power to develop a deeper, more connected silence than one can sometimes achieve alone. The act of going into the center and then out again was a wonderful metaphor for the journey of going inward to receive sustenance from the Holy and returning refreshed to the world that I experience when I meditate deeply.

THE BIBLE CONTAINS STORIES about people journeying toward wholeness. It is a story of people who catch glimpses of what that wholeness could be like, and it is full of stories about people who keep making mistakes. But most of all it is about God's grace. It is about God's incredible intervention in the ways of the world in the life, death, and resurrection of Jesus Christ.

In this story, a man had been an invalid for thirty-eight years. That's a long time. Jesus asks the man a strange question. "Do you want to be made well?" It seems obvious that the man wants to get well. The man answers Jesus, "I can't get to the waters of healing, because everyone is pushing me out of the way." Then Jesus says, "Get up and walk." I wonder what tone of voice Jesus used when he said this. On the one hand, he could have been encouraging, "Come on, now, you can do it, I know you can." Jesus could have been annoyed. He could have been annoyed that nobody helped the man for thirty-eight years. On the other hand, he could have been annoyed at the man for not getting on with his life and allowing his hypochondria to keep him from being whole.

I imagine that Jesus took compassion on the man and healed him on the spot. I wonder what the man did with his life after that! Did he go back to his old ways? Or did he set about on new paths? Did he change his behavior?

Jesus' question to the man is also his question to us. "Do you want to be made well?" Do you want to be whole? But what does that mean? Growing in wholeness means growing in our relationship to God. It means growing in our relationship with one another. It means growing in relationship with all of God's children, including the animals. It means living in harmony with all of God's creation.

Jesus gave us the new vision, the new covenant, the new creation. Jesus showed us God's dream for creation. In God's dream for creation, no one is to be left out. We are not to judge who may or may not belong to God's community.

If we answer Jesus, "Yes, I want to be well," we may have to get up and walk.

As you walk the labyrinth today, hear Jesus asking you, "Do you want to be well?" Don't answer Jesus until you reach the center of the labyrinth. Then if your answer is, "Yes, I want to be well," get up and walk out of the labyrinth a new person ready to live God's dream for creation.

Prayer

O Great and Holy One, guide my feet as I get up and walk today.

I WALKED WITH HIM,
AND I TALKED WITH HIM

John 20:11–18

But Mary stood weeping outside the tomb. As she wept, she bent over to look into the tomb; and she saw two angels in white, sitting where the body of Jesus had been lying, one at the head and the other at the feet. They said to her, "Woman, why are you weeping?" She said to them, "They have taken away my Lord, and I do not know where they have laid him." When she had said this, she turned around and saw Jesus standing there, but she did not know that it was Jesus. Jesus said to her, "Woman, why are you weeping? Whom are you looking for?" Supposing him to be the gardener, she said to him, "Sir, if you have carried him away, tell me where you have laid him, and I will take him away." Jesus said to her, "Mary!" She turned and said to him in Hebrew, "Rabbouni!" (which means Teacher). Jesus said to her, "Do not hold on to me, because I have not yet ascended to the Father. But go to my brothers and say to them, 'I am ascending to my Father and your Father, to my God and your God.'" Mary Magdalene went and announced to the disciples, "I have seen the Lord"; and she told them that he had said these things to her.

Maybe it was the weather. A perfect summer's day, clear and breezy. Surely the location helped. A field overlooking a valley in Western Massachusetts. But I think it was the idea of walking through a labyrinth of lavender that shaped my mood most.

The labyrinth itself sat a little unkempt at the base of the field. I liked that. I was feeling slightly in disarray myself. The lavender bloom was uneven, too, again matching my mindset. So I felt at home as I began my circular walk toward the center.

Not being a regular walker of labyrinths, I had no expectations about being spiritually moved. However, I soon found my mood brightening. I noticed more, thought less. What lavender there was smelled ever so sweet, and the clusters of purple appealed to the eye. I began to hear goldfinches singing in flight. The more I walked, the more I relaxed and became attuned to the landscape. It felt good.

At the center I paused just long enough to take in the outer and inner panoramas. A few deep breaths and thank-yous later, I began retracing my steps. No doubt about it, I felt quite refreshed and calmed after that walk. In my garden, a lavender plant is now flourishing.

WHENEVER I ASK PEOPLE who have to plan a funeral service for their loved one what hymns they would like, most of the time they want "In the Garden." This is especially true of people who rarely come to church. I have to wonder what this is about. There was a time in my denomination when "In the Garden" was on the "Do not sing list." I'm not sure why this was true either. I think it had something to do with the perception that the words to this particular hymn were too romantic. Finally, someone analyzed the words and discovered that they speak of Mary Magdala's experience meeting Jesus after the crucifixion.

Jesus had been executed. All hopes had been dashed. And yet God comes through once again. Not only had the stone been rolled away, but the wall that had surrounded Mary in her grief had been rent open. Jesus came to her in the garden. They walked and they talked. Mary had a transcendent experience, a holy moment. She experienced absolute and total joy.

I think the reason so many choose this hymn to be sung at our beloveds' funerals is that we catch a glimpse of God through Mary's experience as told to us by C. Austin Miles in 1912. And we want it too. We want Jesus to walk with us. We want Jesus to talk with us. We want to feel that exquisite joy that Mary experienced and I expect Miles experienced. In our grief, we can let go, we can let part of the wall that separates us from each other and from God fall down. We can look through the cracks into heaven. We can even allow ourselves to let the Holy Spirit surround us and hold us as if in the hollow of God's hand. We can stop being analytical for a few days. We can allow for the possibility of God. We yearn for this hymn to be our story. As we sing through the tears of our pain and grief, we are also singing about our longing to walk with Jesus and to talk with Jesus.

The Good News is that we don't have to wait for someone to die before we can let go, before we can tear down the walls that separate us from each other and from God. Today is the day to sing. Today is the day to walk and talk with Jesus. Today is the day to experience the intense sweetness of pure joy.

I come to the garden alone,
While the dew is still on the roses;
And the voice I hear, falling on my ear,
The Son of God discloses.

And he walks with me, and he talks with me,
And he tells me I am his own,
And the joy we share as we tarry there,
None other has ever known.

He speaks, and the sound of his voice is so
      sweet
The birds hush their singing;
And the melody that he gave to me
Within my heart is ringing.

And he walks with me, and he talks with me,
And he tells me I am his own,
And the joy we share as we tarry there,
None other has ever known.

I'd stay in the garden with him,
Though the night around me be falling;
But he bids me go;
Through the voice of woe
His voice to me is calling.

And he walks with me, and he talks with me,
And he tells me I am his own,

And the joy we share as we tarry there,
None other has ever known.

As you walk the labyrinth today, sing or say the words "And he walks with me, and he talks with me, And he tells me I am his own, And the joy we share as we tarry there, None other has ever known."

Prayer

O Holy and most Gracious God, thank you.

ACKNOWLEDGMENTS

Over the decades, I have read many books, heard many sermons, and have participated in many workshops. I have heard many people's stories. In this book I present a synthesis of what I have heard, read, and experienced. Some of it may sound familiar to you. I do not claim that anything I have written is mine. I cannot account for where the thoughts came from. At four o'clock in the morning, I just write down what is streaming by in my subconscious. Many people have helped me with this book by sharing their stories of walking the labyrinth and by allowing me to share their stories with you. I am listing their names alphabetically. The stories are all equally important and the pilgrims equally special. Thank you. Thank you. Thank you. And keep walking.

Charlie Camp	Nancy Luce
Roy M. Carlisle	Savanna Ouellette
Barbara Conn	Lois Pinton
Dorothy Cresswell	Donna Schaper
Kay Frye	Pet Stearn
Joan Lindeman	Katie Tolles

ABOUT THE AUTHOR

Carole Ann Camp is a retired ordained minister in the United Church of Christ. She has served several churches in Western Massachusetts as pastor. She holds an M.Div. degree from Andover Newton Theological School and an Ed.D. from the University of Massachusetts. She is co-author of *Labyrinths from the Outside In.*

A WORD FROM
THE EDITOR

Putting each foot down gingerly was having this odd effect on me. It was the first time I had ever walked the labyrinth at Grace Cathedral in San Francisco, and random thoughts were flitting through my brain. Initially I noticed the movement of my feet. I seemed a bit unsteady, but I was trying to walk carefully and slowly and that helped me stay aware of my whole body. I had learned to pay attention to my feet and my style of walking from a wonderful author and friend, Carolyn Braddock (*Body Voices: Using the Power of Breath, Sound, and Movement to Heal and Create New Boundaries*). Years earlier she had tried to help me understand how my style of walking could indicate other psychological issues in my life. She was right. But in this case of walking the path of the labyrinth I was becoming aware of my body and the spiritual issues in my life.

Also, I was aware of how trying to stay on this narrow path and walk deliberately was unexpectedly alerting me to specific thoughts and feelings about spiritual concerns. I was beginning to understand why it was a spiritual exercise; the physical movement was opening up my heart and the deliberate walking was making me stay very present in the moment. It reminded me of something C. S. Lewis had said decades earlier when he discussed prayer. He talked about how kneeling in prayer had its effect on your soul and your attitude. The body is always involved in any spiritual exercise. I did find myself trying to overcome just a whiff of a remnant of my former evangelical orientation toward spirituality where I ignored my body as if it didn't really exist and the only thing that mattered spiritually was what I thought. My years as an Episcopalian had almost rooted out all of that erroneous understanding of spirituality, but there was just this hint of it left.

But now I began to understand that walking the labyrinth was going to be one of the final spiritual exercises to help me fully embrace a present-moment-body-oriented spirituality. It was a subtle but profound next step in my thinking about spirituality and in my own personal spiritual practice. And it also meant that the labyrinth would become a permanent part of my walk toward God and a way to enter into my own inner landscape, where I found subtle perceptions of the Spirit within.

For a long time I could not easily put any of this new understanding or experience into words. So I began to read books on the labyrinth, talk about it with others, even edit and publish a wonderful book by a labyrinth architect (*Labyrinths: Walking Toward the Center* by Gernot Candolini with a foreword by Paula D'Arcy) about its salutary spiritual effects. Easy access to the Grace Cathedral labyrinths, which was a center for the blossoming ministry of the use of the labyrinth around the country and the world, made it easy for me to do this regularly and helped further my own understanding of how this practice was affecting me. Grace had a wonderful indoor labyrinth and an outdoor one that could be walked any time of the day or night. It was modeled on the famous Chartres Cathedral labyrinth, and its form became a standard for most of the labyrinths used throughout the country. This ancient practice was now suddenly being "discovered" and used in most denominations and in many retreats and conferences. Many were finding how powerful and mysterious this activity could be in expanding and enhancing their relationship with God.

I saw many books and articles being published but none of them did what I eventually desired for my own practice. I longed for a meditative book that could be used while you were actually walking the cycles of the labyrinth. It would be a book of thoughtful and helpful meditations which would spur deeper reflections for each individual that used the book and it would not just be a book *about* the labyrinth.

Finally I decided I needed to commission such a book since no one seemed to be publishing what I wanted. In one of those surprising but fortuitous meetings I happened to mention this desire to an agent friend, Linda Roghaar, and she had just the right person for the project. Carole Ann Camp had already co-authored one book on the labyrinth, and when we finally met in person she was enthusiastic about taking on the project. Over a couple of years we met a few times and slowly but surely sorted out what I wanted this book to be. Carole captured my vision superbly, expanded it creatively, and even allowed me to contribute a few of my own stories of walking the labyrinth. This turned out to be one of those wonderful collaborations that produces something better and more helpful than any of the parties involved had anticipated. It pleases me greatly to be able to hold this book in my hands, and I hope the same will be true for you.

Roy M. Carlisle
Senior Editor

Of Related Interest

Dean Brackley, S.J.
THE CALL TO DISCERNMENT
IN TROUBLED TIMES
New Perspectives on the
Transformative Wisdom of
Ignatius of Loyola

As the centerpiece of Crossroad's expanding offerings in Jesuit spirituality and thought, we offer this remarkable book from Dean Brackley, a leader in social justice movements and professor in El Salvador. Brackley takes us through the famous Ignatian exercises, showing that they involve not only private religious experience but also a social, moral dimension, including the care for others.

0-8245-2268-0, $24.95 paperback

Check your local bookstore for availability.
To order directly from the publisher,
please call 1-800-707-0670 for Customer Service
or visit our Web site at *www.cpcbooks.com*.
For catalog orders, please send your request to the address below.

www.crossroadpublishing.com

All prices subject to change.

crossroad